★ THE ★
25TH ANNIVERSARY COLLECTION

Table of Contents

5   **INTRODUCTION**

6   **CHAPTER 1:** HOW WE'VE GROWN
There's a first time for everything, and so many
wonderful ones happen during childhood. First
step, first day of school, first job, first kiss...these
growing-up milestones make lasting impressions
that keep us forever young.

28   **CHAPTER 2:** ALL IN GOOD FUN
All work and no play? No way! Whether it's
catching a pop fly, pitching horseshoes or simply
doing something goofy, there's nothing like good
clean fun to boost the spirit while you're having
the time of your life.

46   **CHAPTER 3:** OUR COUNTRY
The story of America is best told by the people
who built, defended and cherished it. Men and
women in the military, patriots on the homefront
and immigrants who crossed an ocean for a
dream—their words embody the faith, hope and
freedom that have made this nation great.

70   **CHAPTER 4:** TRUE ROMANCE
It's said the course of true love seldom runs
smoothly; it's more like a wild ride! Dating,
weddings and married life rarely go off without a
hitch—which results in some incredibly engaging
recollections shared by readers.

92   **CHAPTER 5:** WHERE THE HEART IS
A house provides shelter, but a home is where
we weather life's little storms and bask in the
sunshine. More than brick and mortar, it's
a kitchen table, a garden, a backyard and a
community of people who love us.

110   **CHAPTER 6:** GETTING BY IN TOUGH TIMES
The hard truths of the Great Depression didn't
harden the American people. In fact, folks
responded with a kindness, ingenuity and heroism
that money can't buy. Wardrobes were made with
feed sacks, debts were forgiven, and hearts and
doors were opened to strangers.

128   **CHAPTER 7:** LET'S CELEBRATE
From New Year's Day through Christmas, the
calendar is dotted with holidays and occasions
steeped in family traditions. These beloved
customs leave us with treasured memories
and have us counting the days until it's time
to celebrate all over again.

148   **CHAPTER 8:** COME ALONG FOR THE RIDE
Get your motor running! Join our caravan of
classic cars, trains, trolleys and other vintage
vehicles that have kept us cruising through the
decades and fueled our thirst for adventure.

168   **CHAPTER 9:** THE WAY WE WERE
Camping out atop flagpoles and cramming into
phone booths...every generation is raging to be
different. We're defined by hairstyles, clothes and
moments in history that forever changed us.

186   **CHAPTER 10:** THAT'S ENTERTAINMENT
Return to those thrilling days of yesteryear when
radio reigned, movies wooed audiences with
all-star casts, and televisions became a living room
fixture. The glitz and glamour of Hollywood never
shone brighter than during this golden age of
family entertainment.

EDITORIAL

EDITOR-IN-CHIEF Catherine Cassidy
CREATIVE DIRECTOR Howard Greenberg
EDITORIAL OPERATIONS DIRECTOR Kerri Balliet

MANAGING EDITOR/PRINT & DIGITAL BOOKS Mark Hagen
ASSOCIATE CREATIVE DIRECTOR Edwin Robles Jr.

ASSOCIATE EDITORS Sharon Selz, Julie Kuczynski
ART DIRECTOR Raeann Sundholm
LAYOUT DESIGNER Catherine Fletcher
EDITORIAL PRODUCTION MANAGER Dena Ahlers
EDITORIAL PRODUCTION COORDINATOR Jill Banks
COPY CHIEF Deb Warlaumont Mulvey
COPY EDITORS Dulcie Shoener, Mary-Liz Shaw, Joanne Weintraub
EDITORIAL INTERN Michael Welch
EDITORIAL SERVICES ADMINISTRATOR Marie Brannon
EDITORIAL BUSINESS MANAGER Kristy Martin
EDITORIAL BUSINESS ASSOCIATE Samantha Lea Stoeger

EXECUTIVE EDITOR, *REMINISCE* Courtenay Smith
MANAGING EDITOR, *REMINISCE* Kerrie Keegan

BUSINESS

VICE PRESIDENT, PUBLISHER Russell S. Ellis

© 2015 RDA Enthusiast Brands, LLC
1610 N. 2nd St., Suite 102, Milwaukee WI 53212-3906

International Standard Book Number: 978-1-61765-499-2
Library of Congress Control Number: 2015942759
Component Number: 117300047H

TIME FLIES...

And it's no wonder! We've had more fun than we dreamed possible putting together *Reminisce* magazine since it premiered in 1991. As we celebrate our silver anniversary, we realize that the success of this unique magazine proves that at least one thing has stayed the same—the comfort and connection reminiscing brings is timeless.

In *Best of Reminisce: The 25th Anniversary Collection*, we've brought back hundreds of stories and photos our contributors submitted over the history of *Reminisce* and *Reminisce Extra*.

You'll find charming glimpses of childhood, heartwarming stories of romance and recollections of favorite autos. There are real-life reflections on the Great Depression and world-shaking wars, as well as touching tales from brave men and women who gave their all for their country.

Of course, there's plenty of fun to be had as we recall the sports, holidays and fads that delighted us through the decades. Whether you danced to the big bands or grooved to rock 'n' roll, you'll love the section on music. Plus, you can tune in to the golden age of radio and TV, and check out the old-time prices in our collection of vintage ads!

We thank our loyal subscribers for sharing precious pieces of their past. And we remind our next generation of readers: What happens today will become the moments you hold on to forever.

Thanks for the memories!

The editors of *Reminisce* magazine

P.S. One of *Reminisce*'s most popular features involves a fashionable character named Hattie. Inevitably, she loses her heirloom hatpin within the pages of the magazine, and readers have a ball looking for it.

Just for fun, we've hidden a sketch of a hatpin somewhere in this book—and it looks exactly like this:

So grab the kids and grandkids, and join in the hunt. Make a game of it and see who finds the pin fastest. If you simply can't locate it, turn to page 208 for the location. In the meantime, have fun reminiscing!

HAVE TODDLERS, STILL TRAVEL For writer Norma Spring and her photographer husband, Bob, of Bellingham, Washington, chronicling their worldwide adventures has been more than a livelihood—it's been their life. Wherever they wandered, it was only natural that their three children came along, as shown in Bob's photo of Norma skiing with baby Jacquie in northern Washington in 1952.

CHAPTER 1

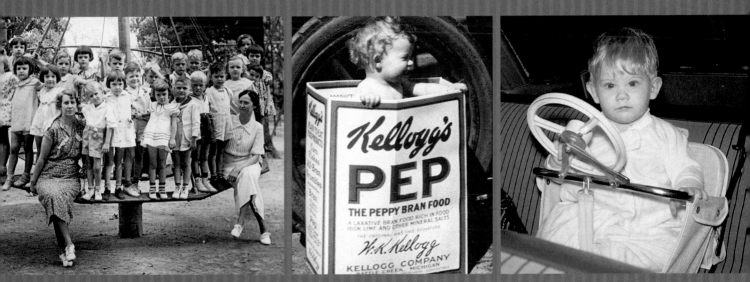

How We've Grown

Remember when we couldn't wait for birthdays to come and seemingly endless school years to go by? Growing up was a jumble of carefree days and butterfly-filled stomachs as we made new friends, amazing discoveries and our share of mistakes on the exhilarating journey to adulthood.

Hey, Baby!

WEE ONES ARE BUNDLES OF FUN

TINY BABY WAS A BIG MORALE BOOSTER

In 1944, my first husband, Elvers Lloyd, and I were living at Camp Blanding, Florida, while he helped train medical personnel for overseas duty.

I'd had a job on the base but gave it up when I became pregnant. While working, I spoke to many soldiers on the phone every day and ate lunch in the mess hall, so I knew a lot of people at camp and continued to see them as I returned to the base hospital for checkups.

All furloughs were frozen, and morale was down as Christmas approached. Elvers took seven soldiers to the main post office in Jacksonville every afternoon to make sure all the mail got to the men at camp before the holiday.

Since my husband was often off base for field training or the mail trips, a sergeant named Nestarick appointed himself my guardian, meeting me at the bus and walking me to the hospital, then back to the bus.

I had met him two years earlier; he'd been in the Army for 30 years and remained there because there were no discharges during the war. He became our on-base grandfather, always ready and waiting to help.

Capt. H.E. Howland, the company commanding officer, left orders that he was to be informed at once when I was admitted. After he got the call at 3:30 a.m. on Dec. 15, word quickly spread, and a few friendly bets were waged.

Our son, Wally, arrived that day at 4:50 p.m., weighing 5 pounds, 2 ounces, as his father tried to read the newspaper in the waiting room. When the nurse called the admittance office about the Lloyd baby, the soldier on the phone yelled, "Whoopee! It's a boy! Give me my $5!"

Sgt. Nestarick had the mess deliver strawberry ice cream and a gallon of green olives, then found us a radio so we could listen to Christmas carols.

On Christmas morning, as we were getting ready to leave the hospital for home, the base commander, a colonel, appeared. He said he had been hearing about this baby for 10 days and just wanted to see him. I smiled proudly—until he said, "Do you mind if I borrow your baby?"

Well, I did mind. I was a new mom—but he was a colonel. Reluctantly, I agreed. Did this big, gruff man even know how to hold a baby?

He wasn't gone long, but it seemed like an eternity to this nervous mother. When he brought Wally back, he thanked me and said, "You'll never know how much this meant." I later learned that he had taken my baby for his wife to hold. Their only son was in a Japanese prison camp.

My baby, of course, had no idea how much he did for so many people just by being born in that Christmas season of 1944. Great things come in small packages, like another small package delivered in a stable so long ago.

DORIS LLOYD SALAT WEST FINLEY, PA

MORALE BOOSTER Little Wally (at top) was born on an Army base at Christmastime in 1944 to Doris and Elvers (above). His birth was a small blessing to many war-weary people on base.

WATTLE HER NAME BE? Betty Ratcliff (a year old at left and third from right above with her family) was shocked, then proud that her mother (second from left) had named her after an unusual friend.

WILL THE REAL BETTY PLEASE STAND UP?

After I was born at Charity Hospital in New Orleans, my mother named me Betty. Growing up in the 1950s, I was always proud to be called that. Mother had a dear older sister by that name, and I became very close to my Auntie Betty.

My pride only grew when I learned that my father had a sister named Elizabeth, and that they called her Betty, too. I felt blessed by both sides of our wonderful family. Talk about building a little girl's self-esteem!

Then, one day when I was grown, my mother revealed the true story of how I got my name. She explained that she had not named me after my dear sweet little aunt. No, she had named me after a chicken!

When Betty was a baby chick, she ate from Mother's hand and followed her around the yard. Later, as a hen, Betty rose up politely from her roost and allowed my mother to gather eggs without so much as a squawk.

Unlike the other hens, she never pecked or scratched when Mother gathered eggs. My heart swelled with pride when I heard my mother speak with such love of her special pet. She explained that Betty was a Rhode Island Red, and she made it sound like royalty. Betty was no snob, though. She loved my mother as much as Mother loved her.

So that was how my mother came to honor me, her precious new daughter, with the name of a dear old friend. To this day, I'm proud to be Betty, the girl who was named for a chicken.

BETTY RATCLIFF ANN ARBOR, MI

"Compare this car seat that my son Glenn, then 11 months, was using in 1962 to those of today. It was important to have a car seat with a steering wheel and horn, and the seat had to be high enough so the child could look out. That's Glenn's brother Mark and sister Kayleen beside him."

TRUDI ALEXANDER JACKSONVILLE, FL

ILLEGAL FISHING ▶
"This picture of my husband, Al, was likely taken for his first birthday, in 1929," writes Lois Emerson of Demotte, Indiana. "He was the first grandchild in his mother's big family, on the southeast side of Chicago. By the way, Al still likes to fish."

◀ ONE PEPPY BABY
We've heard of premiums in cereal boxes, but this tops them all. Marcia Diez of Crystal River, Florida, was just a toddler when she climbed into this giant box of Pep in 1924. Her father was a salesman who set up product displays in stores. One day at home, as her father was unloading his car, Marcia climbed into this bran cereal display box and her mother took the photo. It's often said that kids are full of pep—but this is one case when the Pep was full of a kid!

◀ BABIES WERE BOOMING

Real-life evidence that the war was over and the boys had come home fills this photo taken on Dorothea Williams' front porch on her daughter Wendy's first birthday, March 14, 1947. "From left, the babies are Carol Waranietz, Gary Klima, Wendy, Linda Henriksen, Barbara Williams, Steven Mann and Douglas Honsinger," says Dorothea, of Richmond, California. "Besides my daughter, all were nieces and nephews except one, a cousin to one of the babies. Another niece, Susan, was sick and couldn't make the party. All of the babies were born between March 14 and Dec. 4—quite a production year for our family."

◀ IT'S A WHOPPER, PAPA!

"In 1913, my father, Austin Merrick, and my mother, Annie Howell Merrick, lived and farmed near Big Spring, Texas," writes Edna Teates of Mechanicsville, Virginia. "That's me in a photograph taken at the Howard County fair, posing proudly with a blue-ribbon watermelon my father grew."

Kid Stuff

ENJOYING LIFE'S LITTLE PLEASURES

LEARNING THE ROPES ON A TREELESS TREE HOUSE

It all started one sweltering summer day in 1961 when a big truck pulled up at our house. Two men off-loaded a huge telephone pole, hauled it into the backyard, set it down and left. Mom, whose hands were eternally in hot sudsy, dishwater, looked up from the kitchen sink and wondered if there'd been some mistake. In a corner of the yard, we already had a pole that seemed to be doing a fine job of holding up the tangle of telephone wires.

She called Dad, who said he was glad to hear the thing had arrived safely and to leave it there for him—as if she were intending to roll it away!

Next thing we knew, another truck pulled up. Two guys emerged to dig a deep hole for the telephone pole and secure it with buckets of cement. It stood there like a solemn statue in back of our house.

We went outside and began to gravitate toward the mysterious pole in a way that would later remind me of those apes checking out the monolith in *2001: A Space Odyssey*. We couldn't imagine what plans Dad had for it, but he worked many nights on his architectural notes and sketches.

PLAYING TELEPHONE In 1961, *Parade* magazine gave national attention to the creation enjoyed by Sandy Cares and her siblings. The "tree house" eventually had to come down from overuse, but later the family's youngest brother made a duplicate for his kids.

The towering results of his design and construction labors are in the picture (opposite). The lower platform was about 10 or 12 feet aboveground; the smaller, higher one—he called it the crow's nest—had a trap door for access. The final step was attaching a canvas skull-and-crossbones pennant he'd made to the tip-top of the pole, to the cheers and huzzahs of the neighbor kids.

When our telephone pole tree house was finally ready, we asked, "How do we get up there?"

"You have to climb the rope," Dad told us matter-of-factly, pointing to the thick line that was suspended from a beam halfway up the pole. He demonstrated how to hoist yourself up onto the rope and pull yourself up while gripping it with your hands, feet and legs. We spent the rest of the summer playing pirates.

One night, Dad came home, looked up and angrily demanded to know who had put our 2-year-old sister on the lower platform. No one fessed up, so he sent our friends home and called us inside the house, bringing Martha down himself. We hadn't really noticed she was up there until Dad called to us, and someone said, "She must have climbed the rope herself."

Dad said he would take us at our word (by which he meant smoke us out), and then took our toddler sister back outside and handed her the rope. Then, in front of Dad and the rest of us, Martha took the thick rope in her chubby little baby hands and dragged herself up, up, up, her tiny knees and feet gripping the rope and her cloth diaper drooping behind as she made her way to the platform.

The smile that came to my father's face at seeing this astonishing accomplishment was a great relief to us all. We would never lie to Dad!

SANDY CARES GRAND RAPIDS, MI

SKIPPIN' SISTERS
"My sisters and I were thrilled to appear on the TV series *Stairway to Stardom* in 1951," says Virginia Hormell Patterson of Plains, Kansas. "We won a brand-new Hudson Hornet for tap-dancing with our jump ropes."

▲ **HAPPY CAMPERS**
"My daughter Janice (far right) and her friend Carol Lee are bidding good night to their sisters in 1959," John Spangler, of Hanover, Pennsylvania, writes about the pajama-clad adventurers.

TALK TO ME, DOLLY ➤
Lillian James of Camarillo, California, was tickled with the talking doll her brother, Joe, won in 1926 for getting new customers on his paper route. Cylinder records and a player in the doll's back gave it a voice.

▲ **REAL FISH STORY**
"Knowing how I longed to catch a trout, Dad put one he'd caught on my hook when I wasn't looking," says Stan Zaremba Jr. of Vernon, Connecticut (shown above with sister Joan in 1959).

◄ HERE'S THE SCOOP

"Considering my father owned a large ice cream manufacturing business and we had a complete soda fountain in our basement, it's no wonder I was popular among classmates," writes Russell Ives Jr. of Austin, Texas. "In this photo, Dad is giving two happy kids a free sample during a plant tour in 1950."

▲ FOUR FOR THE DERBY

"My brothers and I entered our local Soap Box Derby in 1938, thanks to sponsors who paid for our wheels," says Richard Aeder (second from left) of Akron, Michigan. "We later used the carts to peddle Mom's bread to help out during the Depression."

School Days

MAKING THE GRADE TOGETHER

DAD PUT A SONG IN HER HEART

It was 1947, and I stood teary-eyed in front of my dad, Edwin Hart. For weeks, two other wannabe high school song leaders and I had been practicing our new routine.

Two of our trio caught on immediately; then there was me. I just couldn't seem to figure things out.

So here we were. My father sat on our front porch while I positioned myself under a palm tree in our front yard.

"Now show me what you can do," he said.

Brow furrowed, I tried to concentrate on my strut. *Need to kick higher, higher,* I told myself. Leaders from Jordan High School in Long Beach, California, were known for that.

Dad interrupted: "Say, Pat, if I'm in the audience and I see you worried over your steps, then I'm not having fun. I don't care about exact steps. I do care if you're having fun.

"Now try again. And let's see a smile. That's it!"

On the day of tryouts, Dad came along with me. As each group stepped up to compete, I saw him watching with intense interest, his fingers gripping the wire fence.

When we were finished, I ran to ask his opinion. He told me our group would win—and he was right. It was a proud moment for a 16-year-old girl to be voted to lead high school songs and cheers. But what was most remarkable to me was that my father, who was recovering from tuberculosis, had walked 3 miles to see me compete.

Song leaders come and go, but who can replace a father like that?

PATRICIA EDWARDS LAKEWOOD, CA

LOVING DAD
Always close to her father, Edwin Hart, Patricia Edwards says she cherishes the fact that "he gave me his time and his love."

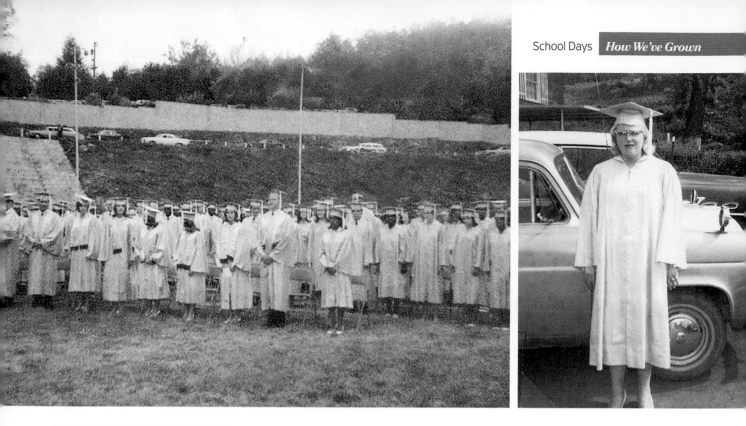

GRADUATION DOWNPOUR WAS A MIXED BLESSING

June 5, 1966, was a bright West Virginia day full of sunshine. It was also the day I had looked forward to all my life: I was a member of the graduating class of Mount Hope High School.

I don't know whose brilliant idea it was for us to hold the graduation ceremony on the school's football field instead of in the auditorium. But there we finally were, marching dutifully to our seats together.

I remember that I wasn't nervous, or at least not much, as the sun gleamed off our shiny gold rented caps and gowns. I spotted my parents, Rachel and Basil, my six siblings and even my grandmother in the center-front bleachers. My father was snapping away with the new flash camera he had bought with his coal miner's wages.

We'd taken our places in front of our chairs and were ready to be seated. Without warning, the skies let loose a drenching cloudburst. Everyone in the class, along with the spectators, scrambled for cover, all except the poor soul who was desperately trying to cover up the piano in the middle of the field.

We would-be graduates made our way to a nearby office building, where we wrung out our soaked gowns and removed the white tassels from our caps. As quickly as it had started, the rain stopped. I looked out the window for a rainbow but saw none.

Strangely enough, it rained nowhere else in the area that afternoon except on our town.

Someone came to tell us that, since the football field was muddy and the bleachers wet, we would graduate in the auditorium after all. To make up for the unpredicted rain delay, we'd have to wear the clothes we had on under our gowns.

Two of my friends, Freeda Coy and Sue Bolen, and I walked to the auditorium in our muddy, waterlogged white shoes. Also, my brand-new dry-clean-only dress was beginning to dry and shrink.

I pulled and tugged, trying to stretch it back to its original dimensions. I was not the only one having this problem. We girls, and some of our mothers, were inadvertently modeling some of the first miniskirts!

Then my wise, unflappable father stood up in his wrinkled shirt and pants to face me. He laughed and spoke these comforting words: "Look around you. Look at all these people who are seated here now."

I did, and that's when I saw the real rainbow. I laughed, too. The social, economic, racial and ethnic boundaries that usually separated us had dissolved in the rain. Our clothes and hairstyles had been leveled—and disheveled—by one great force. Now we were all there for one event, some to close this chapter in our lives by graduating, others to watch loved ones turn to the next page in their future.

"Think of it this way," my father told me. "If it hadn't rained, you would have been just another graduating class, which would fade into memory. Now there's no way anyone here will ever forget the Class of 1966."

Thankfully, Dad had time to snap a shot of me in my gown before the rains came (above, right) and one of our class—complete with streaks caused by a slightly soggy roll of film.

DONNA McGUIRE TANNER OCALA, FL

KEEPING ROMANCE AFLOAT ➤

Water has always had a way of buoying her spirits, writes Camille LeFevre of Estero, Florida. "During our childhood, our grandfather would take my sister and me to the seashore in the summertime. We loved the scent of the ocean as we neared our destination," she says. "I thought it was fitting that the theme of the Vineland (New Jersey) High School junior-senior prom in 1960 was the sea. My date, Maxim, who later became my husband, was in the Navy at the time, so he wore his uniform to the dance. After retiring, we made Florida our home, settling close to beautiful Gulf of Mexico beaches."

◄ A CHEERFUL LEGACY

You can practically hear the *sis-boom-bah* in this shot of Pamela Townsend's mother-in-law, Wilma. "She was a high school cheerleader in the early 1930s," says Pamela, of Spencerville, Ohio. At that time, the megaphone was a key part of a cheerleader's uniform, used to organize the crowd to shout in sync. And since routines were less athletic back then, long skirts and heels didn't cramp their style a bit.

▲ **PEP-TALKING**
True spirit was spelled out by this 1940-'41 elementary school pep team. "Our halftime formations to music at the basketball games always ended with our letters spelling out our little Minnesota town," says Delores Birkholz Gustafson, now of Colorado Springs, Colorado (third from right). "I still have the O and R I wore on front and back."

▲ **BRILLIANT BALANCING ACT**
This 1936-'37 Martin, Tennessee, kindergarten class posed on a suspended merry-go-round with its teachers. "Politeness was just a natural part of our lives," notes Patsy Smith of Muskegon, Michigan (far right, second from top).

That Awkward Age

Let's face it: They don't call them growing pains for nothing. At least looking back on our younger years—as embarrassing as they may have been—is good for a laugh and a sigh of relief.

▲ ALL EARS

"Remember Cracker Jack and the prizes inside?" writes Rosalen Becker of Middle Village, New York. "This is my son Jim in 1951, when he was 4½, wearing one of those prizes." There was no mention of whether Jim's listening improved or not.

▲ TRIBULATIONS OF A TOMBOY

"Every time it snowed in Keyser, West Virginia, my mother, Phyllis Sanders, would put on her brother Dick's knickers and sweater, grab his sled and go sliding down the street," Susan Wilson of Cumberland, Maryland, says about this 1934 photo. Dick secretly complained to their mother that Phyllis was making "bumps" in his sweaters. "When Mom heard this, she was so embarrassed she never wore Dick's clothes again, and he never could figure out why."

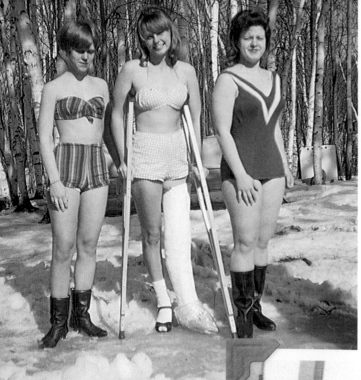

"My daughter Andrea broke her leg during high school gym class in 1966. She and her friends Jane Rostad (right) and Sue Swanson were spending some time at my parents' cabin and decided it would be fun to go out in the snow in their bathing suits. They didn't visit the lake, however, as that was downhill from the cabin."

RUTH WIBERG IRON RIVER, WI

UNDIES MALFUNCTION ➤
"My cousin Ruth (right) and I happily modeled our pretty pink homemade dresses in 1934 while Mom took a picture," says Helen Nelson, Riverside, California. "Later, I was mortified to see one leg of my panties had fallen down when the elastic broke."

◄ GREASY KID STUFF WAS SLICK
"On his way to school, my nephew Richard Tate would stop at our house to 'butch wax' his hair," says Esther McGraw of Hudson, New Hampshire. "In 1960, I snapped him sitting between my son, Mike, and daughter, Ellen. His modified crew cut was called a Hollywood. Today, I think he's glad he has photographic proof that he once had that much hair."

Coming of Age
MARKING MEMORABLE MILESTONES

BANANA SPLIT PERSONALITIES

It was partly the hallway chatter about drive-in movies and partly the gorgeous girls hanging around guys with cars, but I knew that before my senior year in high school, my life had to change: I had to get my first job and some wheels.

Standing on a corner in downtown Paducah, Kentucky, one summer day in 1950, I had no idea where to start. Then I saw the shiny storefront of a Walgreens. As the breakfast crowd thinned out, I asked a man clearing tables in a neat green cap whom I should see about getting a job there.

It turned out to be just the break I needed. The restaurant section of the drugstore was short on workers, and I was hired immediately as a soda jerk. My duties were simple: Wait on customers to their satisfaction and serve them the best food a soda fountain could offer.

Walgreens often ran spring and summer specials, one of which was the July Banana Split. To drum up sales, management would award $10 to the soda jerk who moved the most splits. During these two-week specials, we made sure to give extra-flowery descriptions of our ice cream delicacies.

As the final Friday night of the summer contest unfolded, my partner, Charlene, was leading the pack in sales. The crowds from nearby movie theaters were massive. We were set for a showdown!

Charlene and I were slugging it out, selling sundaes left and right. The movies had just let out, and we were packed to the rail with customers.

In one last charge, Charlene sold six banana splits. With two in each hand and one resting on each arm, she came marching down the freshly mopped floor. Then, without warning, her feet slipped out from under her, and everything came crashing down. As she tried to get up—dripping syrup, whipped cream and three flavors of ice cream—customers cheered and applauded.

Charlene and I eventually got our composure back, but not before we'd laughed ourselves into hysterics. One lesson I learned as a soda jerk was invaluable: Always be able to laugh at your mistakes.

BLANTON CROFT HAGERSTOWN, MD

BIG CHILL Thirsty customers tested the sales skills of soda jerk Blanton Croft (above).

EATING ICE CREAM: BETTMANN/CORBIS

SALUTING SIBLINGS
Each Sunday, Coy Watson (playing the bugle) would call his brothers and sisters together for a flag-raising at their home. Their ritual sent waves of patriotism throughout their neighborhood.

FAMILY ALLEGIANCE

As far back as I can remember, Mom and Dad taught us kids to love God and our country and to be proud of the American flag that we flew over our modest Los Angeles home.

I learned of the birth and history of Old Glory from my copy of *The Boy Scout Handbook*. As soon as my younger sisters and brothers were old enough, I told them the story.

It was with pride that every Sunday morning, after we kids were dressed and ready for Sunday school, we lined up in the front yard to raise our flag in a serious patriotic ceremony.

Our little patrol of seven stood at rigid attention, holding a salute. Then I'd take a deep breath and blow into my $4 brass bugle. All eyes followed the Stars and Stripes upward as our color guard pulled the lines briskly, raising our flag to the top of a 10-foot pole.

My sister Vivian led us in the Pledge of Allegiance, which was known even by my 4-year-old brother, Delmar. Then, at Vivian's command, the saluting hands dropped smartly to our sides. Dismissed, we broke ranks and were off to church.

Often, we'd get a wave of approval from our neighbors across the street. Sometimes, even folks walking by on their way to church would stop and watch, taking off their hats to observe the ceremony. They'd tell us they liked what we did. Mom and Dad were proud of us, too, and frequently told us so.

One Sunday morning, to our surprise and delight, a photographer showed up and took a picture of us putting up our flag (above). It appeared in *The Los Angeles Times* on April 29, 1929.

Many times before that day—and many times since—we have honored Old Glory. Looking at this simple photograph brings back the feelings of love and respect our family had for this country and one another.

COY WATSON ALPINE, CA

PERFECT SQUEEZE PLAY

Imagine the sound of 23 accordions playing at once!

I'm second from the right in the front row at this 1951 performance. I recall one of our crowd-pleasing selections was a jazzy rendition of *The Sheik of Araby*. Our director was Dusty Owens (far right). I wonder if he knew I had a big crush on him.

The studio was called the Honolulu Conservatory of Music, but it was in Flint, Michigan, 12 miles from my home in Clio. Every week, I took a Greyhound bus to Flint, walked five blocks to the studio, then climbed the stairs to the third floor. After the lesson, I did it all over again, all the while lugging my big accordion in its case! I have many fond memories of those days.

BARBARA PETH NICHOLAS ORLANDO, FL

BIG BOY'S BIKE "This is me at 8 years old, in 1952, when I lived in rural Decatur County, Indiana," says David Sutton, who now lives in North Vernon. "This was my first bike, and I was so proud of it. I received many scratches on my knees and legs while riding on the gravel roads around our farm, but it was well worth it!"

WIRED FOR CURLS

The summer I turned 7, in 1942, my mom decided
it was time to do something about my hair. Because
it was fairly long and very fine, she scheduled a
perm. I was excited about the prospect of becoming
a dark-haired version of Shirley Temple.

Mom and I walked about six blocks to the
hairdresser's on Rising Sun Avenue on a hot, humid
July day in Philadelphia. The first thing I noticed
in the steamy shop was the smell of the chemicals
that reminded me of rotten eggs.

As we waited our turn, the owner's dog came
over for a sniff, and we really hit it off. She wouldn't
leave my side, even when I began getting my perm.
The hairdresser summoned the photographer from
the shop next door to take this picture (below) to
display in her store window.

Unfortunately, everyone was so interested in
getting the picture taken that no one was paying
attention to the perm. The end result was terrible.
I looked as if I had put my finger in the proverbial
electrical socket. So much for my dreams of
becoming a Shirley Temple look-alike!

JUNE HORNICKLE BENSALEM, PA

Reader Favorites
BROTHERLY LOVE IN A BASEBALL GLOVE

Some years ago, my wife and I were visiting with my youngest brother, Cam. We were out on his patio when the conversation turned to family memories.

I was 9 years old in 1956 when Cam—more formally, William Cameron—was born. Mom had already taught me to change diapers after my other brother, Tracy, was born in 1951. I knew how to slip my finger in the diaper so that the safety pin would stick me and not the infant, and I also knew how to bottle, bathe and burp a baby.

Confident in my abilities, Mom often left me in charge of Tracy and Cam if she had to leave the house briefly.

My dad lost his railroad job in 1958. Work was hard to come by in our part of Tennessee, so when his unemployment ran out, he and Mom decided he'd leave for California to look for a job. Fortunately, he found work, and soon we moved out to California and became a family again.

In 1967, I was about halfway through my tour with the Marine Corps in Vietnam. I got a letter from Cam, who had just turned 11. The note was so simple and direct it gave me and my buddies a good laugh:

Dear Terry, How are you doing? You must not be wounded or dead because Mom hasn't mentioned it.

I am playing Little League ball again this year and need a new glove. Mom and Dad can't afford it. I am still using your old glove. Could you buy me a new one? Love, Cam.

I had been sending money home each month, so I wrote Mom and told her to tap my bank account and take my brother to the sporting goods store to buy the glove he wanted.

When I got home in December, Cam showed me the glove and thanked me. I attended his Little League games for the next few years, and he played his heart out, becoming an all-star shortstop.

One day when I was in the stands, he made a spectacular play to end an inning and ran off the field to the applause of fans from both teams.

We made eye contact, and Cam raised his glove hand skyward. The fans probably thought he was acknowledging them. In fact, he was thanking me for his gift.

When I told this story to the family that night on Cam's patio, he walked into the house and came back minutes later with the glove. He called it his prized possession. Both of his children used the glove when they played baseball themselves, but their dad always cautioned them never to leave it unattended.

As far as we can remember, Cam and I have never had an argument. My changing his diapers and giving him baths must have bonded us for life.

TERRY LEE WILSON PICO RIVERA, CA

KID'S GLOVE Author (at left) paid for the baseball glove little brother Cam used in a '68 all-star game (right). They have been close since Cam was a baby (below, also with brother Tracy).

October 1952

CAUGHT IN THE ACT! "This is a family-favorite photo showing my daughter, Shirley, and her uncle Timmy Smith," says Artye Lee Scott of Spokane, Washington. "That cookie jar featured a lid that was almost impossible to remove without making a telltale 'alarm' sound."

BLOOMING BEAUTY In 1951, Edna Marsh volunteered her green thumb to maintain the Bridge of Flowers in Shelburne Falls, Massachusetts—an abandoned trolley bridge-turned-gorgeous garden path. Edna's friend Judy Teasdale of Naples, Florida, shared the colorful snap.

CHAPTER 2

All in Good Fun

Win, lose or draw—in the game of life, what's really important is having a blast while we're at it. Whatever the hobby, sport, pastime or passion, taking time out to play can transform even the dullest day into a laughing matter.

Good Sports

HERE'S HOW WE PLAYED THE GAME

THE UNDERDOGS

In 1927, the high school in tiny Mount Carmel, Illinois, did the unthinkable, winning the state basketball championship. Big schools from Chicago, Peoria, Springfield and Rockford were all defeated by a little high school in a town on the banks of the Wabash River.

My father, Cliff Garrett (in a suit, above), was the coach of that team and believed strongly in discipline and dedication. He was also superstitious. Before the championship game in Champaign, Dad refused to let his team take the floor. Their lucky uniforms with the maroon letters had been left back at a hotel in nearby Urbana.

The team had another set of uniforms, but they wouldn't do, so Dad arranged a police escort for the student manager and sent him rushing 12 miles back to Urbana. By the time the manager returned, the game had been held up for 20 minutes. But, wearing the lucky uniforms, the Mount Carmel squad took an early lead and held it all the way, stunning Peoria 24 to 18.

Followed by droves of loyal fans, the team arrived back in Mount Carmel at 3 a.m., and the city celebrated the victory on Market Street. Dad eventually moved to Indiana and taught high school for 43 years. But whenever he returned to Mount Carmel, those who remembered that glorious year of 1927 still called him Coach.

JUDY GARRETT GABE EVANSVILLE, IN

PRETTY PITCHERS ➤
"My mom, Anna Rust (far right, front), met my dad while pitching horseshoes in 1929," says Glendora Hammond of Chino Hills, California. "They were both champions."

WOMEN'S CHAMPIONSHIP HORSE SHOE TOURNAMENT. RIVERSIDE PARK COURTS. MOLINE, ILL. AUG. 29- SEPT. 2, 1935.

▲ HI, JUMPER
Orla Jean Williams just had to try the kids' high jump in the yard of her family's Mayfield Heights, Ohio, home in the early '50s. Husband David, who took the photo, set up the pole to help the kids stay in shape–but adults were intrigued by it, too, as Orla Jean's uplifting attempt clearly demonstrates.

"My husband, Joe (next to the coach), and fellow members of the 1932 sprint relay team in Sayre, Oklahoma, were proud of their new warmup uniforms. To me, they look more like prison yardbirds than runners."

ALMA GILLUM CORONADO, CA

TAKING THE PLUNGE ➤

"A friend and I were bitten by the scuba diving bug early," says Bernice Petty Weldon of Loveland, Colorado. "I was 16 years old when this photo of me was taken in 1933 at Alki Beach in Seattle, Washington. The sea diving tank was made from the top of a water heater, and the hose to supply air was connected to a tire pump. We'd carry 50 pounds of weight around our waists when in the water, and we did this from a rowboat at a depth of about 20 feet. We stopped our watery explorations when my friend almost drowned. I was trying to pull him into the boat and pump air to him at the same time."

◄ SUMMER TEE TIME

"My cousin Kai Person snapped his smiling wife, Winifred, as she prepared to hit the links in 1934," says Rose Ingeson from Glenview, Illinois. "A long skirt and casual sweater were considered perfect golfing attire for women back then."

▲ FLIPPING FOR GYMNASTICS

"My mother, Irma Kuchenbecker (fourth from right), was a member of *Turnverein Germania*, an athletic association in Los Angeles," writes Joyce Martinsen of Palos Verdes Estates, California. "This picture was taken in 1925 when she and her teammates were competing at a meet in Louisville, Kentucky." In German, *Turner* means gymnast and *Verein* means club.

◄ HAVING A BIG BALL

Paul Arent from Van Nuys, California, snapped these two plucky youngsters playing a spirited game of soccer with an enormous ball. Paul doesn't recall the boys' names, but one thing's for certain: There can be no excuses for missing a kick!

Pastime Pleasures

HOBBIES THAT HELP THE HEART BEAT

CONFESSIONS OF A CONTEST FANATIC

Before the days of state lotteries, local and national companies sponsored endless contests. Entry blanks were everywhere—in magazines, newspapers and store displays. And for some of us, participation became a fun hobby.

As a young Colorado housewife in 1956, I had entered a Sweetheart Soap Dream Home contest and won my first prize ever: a three-piece set of luggage. A neighbor saw my name on the winners list and invited me to join the local contest club. It was nice to have someone to call after getting a letter that began: "Congratulations! You're a winner!"

Over the years, I won, among other things, a portable hi-fi stereo from Lever Brothers, a sleeping bag from Kool-Aid and sports equipment from Colgate. In a regional appliance dealer's contest, I was delighted to earn a much-needed Philco refrigerator-freezer for extolling the "Four Freedoms" the freezer would provide: freedom from "flint-hard meat, forlorn produce, fretful defrosting and frequent marketing."

A 1957 RCA Whirlpool contest required describing what you liked best about its new washer-dryer. My nearly 100-word entry had a Cinderella theme, ending with "Monday mourning's past—I'll wash happily ever after!" The result was my biggest prize ever: a trip to Paris for my husband and me!

When I began working full time five years later, I had less time for contests. By the '70s, sweepstakes had taken over, and skill wasn't involved anymore. Winning was strictly by the luck of the draw.

That's too bad, because I loved the challenge of polishing words so that my entry stood a chance of catching a judge's eye and meriting a letter that began: "Congratulations! You're a winner!"

BETTY DAY COLORADO SPRINGS, CO

A WAY WITH WORDS Betty Day had a gift for winning contests. Her first prize was a set of luggage (above), which she used when she won a trip for two to Paris (right).

FREE CAMERA MADE THE '30S A SNAP

In 1930, the Eastman Kodak Co. rewarded me for being born—and sparked a long-lasting interest in photography.

Back then, as part of an advertising promotion, Kodak offered all children born in 1918 a free camera and film. What a stroke of luck! I was sure glad to be 12 that year.

I received my Kodak 120 box camera and a free roll of film from Jack Minty, the friendly druggist in Soda Springs, Idaho. Jack did everything from selling prescriptions to assisting the local doctor in operations. He also knew an awful lot about the products he sold. He taught me to hold my breath when I gently pushed the camera's shutter button. He also advised me to take my pictures only on clear days, with the sun at my back. I couldn't wait to get home and try out my new camera!

We lived on a farm along the old Oregon Trail, and I took my first pictures there, snapping anyone and anything that would hold still.

The first photo I took was of my brother Roger next to our pony Dove (below). Brother Lynn graciously posed for my next shot on the back of his pony, Tony (below, middle). Later on,

I snapped a picture of Mother feeding our rabbit (bottom, right).

Of course, no adolescent boy could have resisted taking a picture of his cousin after her first home permanent (middle, right). I can still remember the nasty green mixture Relia Bee used to keep a wave in her hair.

I let my sister Josephine take the last photograph that day (at right). Left to right are me, my sister Jessie, my two brothers and my mother. After that, my parents said enough was enough and called a halt to my incessant shutterbugging for the rest of the day.

I kept that Kodak 120 for about five years, then graduated to a Kodak 116. When I went into the service in 1941, I bought a Brownie Target Six-16. A real workhorse, it took thousands of pictures over the years.

I gave my first little 120 camera to a buddy who was my age but had never gotten a free camera of his own. I hope it brought him as much joy as it brought me during the Depression. We didn't have much in those days, so we took advantage of opportunities we had.

I'll always be thankful to Kodak for helping me capture some precious family moments on film and for sparking my interest in taking pictures—a development that helped me capture and preserve a lifetime of memories.

CARL STODDARD GEORGETOWN, ID

◀ **HAVE THEY GOT A CLUE?**

"I took this photograph on Christmas 1960, after our family got a Clue board game," says John Seiz of Highland Heights, Ohio. "Shown in the photo are my mother, Mary; my sister, Mary; my father, Edwin; and my brother, George." From the slew of tally sheets, it appears the game had been going awhile.

▲ **FIRST FLIGHT**

"The kite I'm holding in 1934, when I was 13, came from trading in cereal box tops," writes Henrietta Meyer Finke from Allison, Iowa. "Advertised as a paper airplane kit, it had a 4-foot wingspan. After I put it together, I found that even the slightest breeze would send this lightweight beauty soaring skyward."

▲ **BOOKS ON WHEELS**

"It was a special event for farm families when the Hennepin County (Minnesota) Library truck made its monthly stop," says Patty Chisel of Big Lake, Minnesota. "On this day in 1937, the truck stopped at my grandparents' store, where eager readers were waiting."

▲ CUTTING CLASS

"I'm the boy on the right in this 1948 photo, taken in the garage of my friend Dennis Finch (far left)," says Charles Eastman from Visalia, California. "We were both 5 years old, and Denny's father, Loren (with saw), took the picture using a timer so he could be in it, too. He developed and printed this in his own darkroom. A career Army master sergeant, he served in Germany during World War II. It warms my heart to think of this patient and generous man making time to teach and share invaluable skills with two inexperienced little helpers."

◄ A TISKET, A TASKET...

Little Kathy's grandfather made the most amazing baskets. "In this photograph, a family favorite, she seems to be saying, 'Show me how to do that,'" Kathy's mother, Pepper Kirtley, from Churubusco, Indiana, writes about the intergenerational lesson. "Kathy was 4 at the time—and today, her home is filled with many cherished items her grandfather lovingly wove for her."

Animal Magnetism

BELOVED CREATURES GREAT AND SMALL

THE DRESS THAT BLACKIE BOUGHT

The screen door slammed shut that Monday morning as Mom carried a bushel basket of damp laundry toward the clothesline on our Missouri farm.

My washday duties included wiping down the old wire clothesline with a damp rag. As I worked, I paused to pet Blackie, Dad's favorite coonhound, who often slept under the tree that held up one end of the line.

Once the laundry was hung, Mom went to prepare lunch while I fled to my swing under the old oak. Meantime, Blackie's ears perked up as he stared at the clothes dancing in the wind. Ambling over to this spectacle, he stopped before a colorful flower-print item: Mom's church dress!

In one split second, Blackie lunged at the flowered dress just as the wind picked up. There was a loud *r-i-i-i-p* as he came away with a large portion of the dress hanging from his wrinkled jowls.

Instantly, Mom let forth a bloodcurdling shriek from the kitchen window. Blackie fled with a yelp, his floral prize still in his mouth, hotly pursued by an irate, rotund woman swinging a broom like an ax.

Hearing Blackie's yelps, Dad flew out of the barn to rescue his hound and ran smack into the gale-force wind that was Mom.

Now she was shaking her broom—and the remains of her Sunday best—at both Dad and his destructive pup.

Nodding his head, Dad slowly backed into the barn, with Blackie cowering behind.

Dinner, usually a lively affair, was somber that day. Dad took Blackie's supper to the safety of the barn.

The week passed in unaccustomed silence until Saturday morning, when we all piled into the car for our weekly trip to town. Parking on the square, each of us went our separate ways: Dad to the feed store, Mom to the dime store and I to the matinee.

Usually Dad shared the news from fellow farmers on the way home, but this time he was quiet. Mom, holding a string-tied package in her lap, just smiled and watched the scenery.

On Sunday morning, Dad and I waited in the car for Mom to join us for the drive to church. My mouth dropped in amazement when she appeared in a brand-new store-bought dress.

Mom settled into her seat with a contented smile. Proudly fingering the imitation pearl buttons on her prize, she said, "Blackie bought it for me."

That afternoon, Dad's best coonhound emerged from his weeklong stay in the barn. Nothing more was ever said about the dress—but every Monday thereafter, Dad and Blackie disappeared into the barn and didn't come out until the clothesline was bare.

JUDI WEBER CARTHAGE, MO

BLACKIE'S FAMILY That's the author with her parents, Earl and Bertha Weber, at top, and Blackie greeting Aunt Ruby below.

HORSE GAVE GRANDPA A RUN FOR HIS MONEY

My wife's grandfather Walter Worrell went to an auction one day around 1903 and purchased a nice-looking horse. Happy with his acquisition, he took the handsome jet-black creature home to show off to his wife, Minnie.

Grandma looked the horse over with a skeptical eye. "Just how much did you pay for this animal?" she asked. When Grandpa shared the price, she said it seemed too low for such a beauty. Grandpa assured her of his horse-trading prowess and suggested they put his bargain to the test.

Agreeing, Grandma fetched their 6-year-old son, Orla, and climbed into the buggy, with Grandpa at the reins. The horse performed well, until another buggy attempted to pass. Instantly, the race was on!

Even after the other buggy was left in the dust, the black horse ran full speed another half-mile. Grandpa had bought himself a former racehorse!

The situation came to a head one day when Grandma was taking Orla to school. Hearing a buggy close behind, the black horse turned into a rocket. As Grandma turned the critter onto Market Street, the carriage careened up on two wheels.

That night, Grandma put her foot down: "Walter, I am not going to be made to look like a floozy, racing around the streets of town, just because of that horse of yours!"

So the next auction day, the big horse was gone. But the story still rears up at every family reunion.

DAYNE SHAW GERMANTOWN, OH

ANY SARDINES IN THERE? ➤

A snap of two cute cat burglars was shared by Kathy Rager of Paterson, New Jersey. "Our dad, John Reid, took this charming 1940 photo of my sisters Mary Ann (left) and Dorothy Marie checking out the icebox for a treat and something for Smokey, our six-toed cat," Kathy writes. "Both girls were wearing the old-fashioned trap-door pajamas that were popular back then. It looks as if Smokey got a taste of good things to come!"

◄ COON DOG ON DUTY

"My brother, Jerry Cornish, is holding our pet raccoon, Cooney, as our dog, Tippy, plays along in 1953, when Jerry was 11," says Michelle Negaard from Vernon Center, Minnesota. "Our pets were great friends. Tippy would stand very still as Cooney put his pointed snout and nose in his ear, as though they were sharing a secret. Cooney weighed almost 40 pounds, likely from all the treats we fed him, and meticulously washed all his food in a pan of water we provided."

▲ BOY'S BEST FRIEND

"This is my favorite photo, circa 1940, of my brother Matt 'Buddy' Waisanen," writes Marion Kaipio of Calumet, Michigan. "The dog, Shep, belonged to our neighbor. Buddy and Shep got the cows in each evening in time for Mother to start milking."

◄ PUPPY LOVE

"Our sons, John (left) and Rick, loaded our latest additions into their wagon in 1952," writes Louella Kightlinger of Erie, Pennsylvania. "John was 5 and Rick, 3." Louella adds that a similar slide of the brothers and the rambunctious litter won a spot on a calendar.

Just for Grins

Some of the most memorable pictures are worth a thousand giggles, at least. From comical candids to silly slides and preposterous portraits, these photos are bound to make you smile.

▲ OPTICAL COLLUSION
"In the late 1950s, I took this wacky shot of my best friend, Joey," says Sheldon Levy, San Francisco, California. "He put his pants and shirt on backward and reversed his shoes. We had everyone fooled until my brother Larry laughingly pointed out the shadow of Joey's head bent down. We couldn't believe we'd missed that detail!"

▲ MULTITASKING AUNTIE
Beautiful hair and child care aren't mutually exclusive, says Carol Burghauser from Baltimore, Maryland. "In this 1964 photograph, my Aunt Francie is reading a favorite story to my cousins Ron (left) and Bob while using her soft bonnet dryer."

➤ A SPOT OF TEA?
Fine silver was brought by toboggan for teatime in 1958 on Mount Cranmore in New Hampshire. Norma Jean Hissong of Olympia, Washington, whose father, Norman, took the photo, says her parents didn't know these genteel people but certainly enjoyed the scene.

▲ SUPERSIZING A STUDE
Weighing 600 pounds, this gigantic wooden Studebaker was built as a prop for a short advertising film around 1930. "My relatives enjoyed posing with it for these fun photos I found in my family album," says Thomas Rzonca, Valparaiso, Indiana.

◄ A COOLA HULA
"Eileen Krause (left) and I were instructors with the Eau Claire (Wisconsin) Figure Skating Club," says Georgia Ione Grilley Murray of Port Charlotte, Florida. "Here, we're preparing for a 1958 show featuring 75 skaters."

➤ HA-HA HATS
A funny hat party in 1954 still brings smiles to hostess Marie Schuessler of Lakewood, New Jersey. One chapeau was more outrageous than the next!

Reader Favorites

MYSTERY MAN TURNS KIDS INTO WINNERS

PLAY BALL!

When I was 7 years old, during the 1930s, there were no playgrounds in the Tioga section of Philadelphia. We'd play two-hand touch football in the street—until the police showed up.

Apparently there was a law against it. I can still see the squad car rounding the corner of Estaugh Street, police officers on the running boards, trying to catch us.

We kids gave up this criminal activity the day a man named Mr. Barnes got permission from the owner of a vacant lot to turn it into a playground.

Mr. Barnes was a quiet, proper gentleman, always wearing a pressed shirt and tie with a dress hat. His only interest seemed to be making sure we kids had a safe place to play. With no help from the city, Mr. Barnes went to businesses in the neighborhood for donations of money or services.

The phone company gave him some old poles for a fence around the lot. Another company lent him a bulldozer and an operator to smooth the field. Several parents, my father included, volunteered their days off to work on the place, building basketball backboards and baseball backstops. Soon there was a huge box stuffed with donated footballs, basketballs, softballs, mitts and bats.

We kids had to contribute, too. Many times, when we arrived to play, Mr. Barnes first made us pick up all the stones on the field.

He also had strict rules of conduct. Fighting and swearing were verboten. We couldn't even say "gee."

There was no Little League or anything else like that. There were no coaches and no parents watching to make sure their kid played enough innings. We just played ball.

During the school year, I'd run home, say hi to my mother, change clothes, run down to the field to play ball, then run home, almost always late for dinner. I'd leave my muddy shoes on the porch, eat, help do the dishes, then run back to play more ball. At dark, I'd run back home and do my homework.

We never knew much about Mr. Barnes. He kept to himself and asked nothing from us other than that we follow his rules. Why he did all of this for us we never found out.

Whatever his reasons, Barnsie's Stadium, as we called it, made life so much more fun for us kids. He will remain in our memories as the man who saved us from the paddy wagon and taught us to practice good sportsmanship always, on the field and off.

JIM JORDAN WEST DES MOINES, IA

TWANG NEEDED TWEAKING "One day we were visiting the family of Karl Wilkinson, who lived in San Jose, California, when I went outside to check on an unusual noise," writes Al Scheuller of Carson City, Nevada. "I ran into this scene, which was a natural for the camera. Arleen Wilkinson is in back, trying to tune out the din. The boys, from left, are Gary Scheuller, Dennis Scheuller (a cousin) and Asil Wilkinson. I was lucky to catch these novice guitar pickers in action!"

GOT HER PROPS "My mother, Pauline Mauck, was crowned Miss Raider of 1944," writes Susan Tooley of Poseyville, Indiana. "She's perched on a P-47 Raider, a plane she helped build as a machine operator at Republic Aviation. This shot attracted many pen pals."

CHAPTER 3

Our Country

❖

When it comes to celebrating the red, white and blue, Americans are proud to show their true colors. From selfless service in wartime to patriotism on the homefront, these stories display an unflagging spirit that's made the American dream a reality for millions the world over.

As You Were

PERIL IN PARADISE

The years before World War II were magical in Hawaii. With few tourist hotels or shopping malls, the islands were sleepy, largely rural places. We'd moved to the Nuuanu Valley to be near Father, a naval officer on the *USS Indianapolis*, the flagship of the Pacific fleet. Only 10 years old in 1941, I understood little of the talk about impending war.

Before putting out to sea in September, Father made arrangements for Mother, my sister and me to sail back to California on Nov. 13 to escape the attack by Japan he feared was imminent. But as soon as Father left, Mother—who felt sure we were in no danger—canceled our reservations. I'll never forget Dec. 7, the day we found out she was wrong.

Running outside to play that Sunday morning, I noticed bits of hot metal in the street, which turned out to be shrapnel from bursting bombs. When I saw planes diving and bombs being dropped, I assumed it was a mock battle. But the Rising Sun emblems on the planes quickly convinced me of the enormity of what was happening.

Mother wasn't at home. She had left a note saying she'd gone off with a neighbor to "watch the war" from a nearby hill. Seldom afraid of anything, she was still sure we'd all be just fine.

I turned on the radio to listen for news, and heard terse messages: "Do not go outside. Don't believe anything you hear until it's been confirmed. Put up blackout curtains."

To our relief, Father and his crew were safely out to sea that morning. Mother, my sister and I soon left the island with only a day's notice, by troopship. We didn't go back to Hawaii until 1946, when Father was made a rear admiral in command of the Pearl Harbor naval shipyard.

Our return was emotional, with all of our old friends coming to greet us at the docks with leis. The war was finally over, we had won, and we were returning at last to our beloved islands.

DORIS SOSIN SANTA MONICA, CA

SAD BUT SMILING Doris Sosin (center below) and her sister (on the left) and mother were all dressed up to leave Hawaii as the war started. Her father (at left), meanwhile, was at sea aboard the *USS Indianapolis*.

THIS BUGLE BOY BLEW IT

When I arrived at the 5th Replacement Depot in Brisbane, Australia, in October 1943, I heard a band playing.

Just 18, and a former high school clarinetist, I met with our outfit's band director, Sgt. Marvin Wadley. I auditioned and was accepted with the words, "You're the new bugler for Company A."

"But Sarge," I protested. "I'm a woodwind player."

"Yes," he agreed. "And you have three weeks to become a bugler."

On the big day, I slowly climbed the ladder to the platform where I was to blow "Assembly" and "Mess Call" into a megaphone. Facing 5,000 soldiers and sweating profusely, I put the bugle to my lips and began blowing the few notes I could manage.

"Shoot the bugler!" they cried.

After the troops tired of jeering, they headed for the mess hall, and I slunk to my tent.

In view of my lackluster performance, I was handed a sax and played with the band until it broke up when our depot was moved to New Guinea. (That's me seated second from left, above.)

After the war, I became a band director. Through 45 years of teaching, I learned that my lips were too thick for the bugle's mouthpiece. I also learned to fit my players to their instruments.

Thanks to a traumatic morning before one tough audience, there were never any one-note horn players in my bands!

BILL PETREMAN MEMPHIS, TN

ARLENE THE FLYING MACHINE

While my uncle Harvey St. Clair served in the Army Air Corps in World War II, he was in charge of a plane that he named *Arlene*, after me. That's Uncle Harvey with the plane (above). I was about 4 years old at the time, and my parents were divorced, so he was a father figure to me.

When Uncle Harvey came home on leave, he told me to pick out whatever I wanted from the Sears book, and he would buy it. I picked out an outfit, and shortly after it came, my mother had a photo (inset) taken of me wearing it.

I chose a naval-looking outfit. I'm sure Uncle Harvey wondered about that, but he never said a word about it. Much later, I even ended up marrying a Navy man!

My uncle passed away in 1946, when I was just 8 years old, but the love, attention and kindness he showed me left a lasting impression—and a wonderful memory.

ARLENE CULROSS SAN JACINTO, CA

FIRST INTRODUCTION ▶

"This picture marks the first time I saw my daughter Barbara, who was born in Philadelphia in March 1944," writes Lewis Benzon of Shrewsbury, Massachusetts. "My wife, Eleanor, followed me all through training from Florida to Ohio and to three bases in California. Then she went home to deliver Barbara. I completed my pilot training in Colorado, was given a seven-day pass and hurried back to Philly, where this picture was taken."

◀ SEASON'S GREETINGS

"We had no Christmas cards to send home when I was with Patton's Third Army on the French-Belgian border in December 1944," says Eugene Mauro from Nutley, New Jersey. "So we made a sign and took pictures of one another standing beside it. We were about to be sent to Bastogne, Belgium, to fight the Battle of the Bulge."

▲ BON VOYAGE!

Nancy Freas of Hatboro, Pennsylvania, writes, "*The Philadelphia Inquirer* gave this 1939 photo of my future parents the following caption: 'Everyone knows that Alex Allison of 510 Howell St. risked falling overboard to give Dorothy Knof of 536 Anchor St. a last goodbye kiss when he left Saturday on a cruise aboard the destroyer *USS Hopkins*. There just is no privacy, what with a photographer and things.'"

◄ YOU'RE IN THE ARMY, KID

Precocious soldier Mel Rudolph of Las Vegas, Nevada (standing second from left), enlisted at age 13. A note from his frantic parents earned the eighth-grader an honorable discharge. He was drafted "for real" in 1952 and served in Korea and Japan.

Women in Uniform
FEMALES JOIN THE FIGHT

WAC PLOWED HER WAY TO SUCCESS

I was living in Tucson, Arizona, when I joined the Women's Auxiliary Army Corps (WAAC) in 1942 and was sent to Fort Des Moines, Iowa, for basic training in the dead of winter. I'll admit the change in climate was tough. But it was easy for me to follow and obey orders, so basic training was a joy.

Proud to be in uniform, I requested assignment to a recruiting office. My wish was granted, and I was transferred to the Chicago office, after skipping over private first class and being promoted to corporal. I attended bond rallies and gave a radio interview. Because of my farm background, I was even chosen to climb aboard a tractor and plow a victory garden (above).

After my recruiting duty, I was sent back to Fort Des Moines, where I helped process a flock of enthusiastic enlistees, sometimes as many as 2,000 women a week.

By that time, the WAAC had become the Women's Army Corps (WAC), converting us from an auxiliary unit into the official women's branch of the Army. A WAC captain interviewed me for my next assignment, which gave me a first-hand understanding of a turning point in world history.

The Oak Ridge (Tennessee) National Laboratory was established in 1943 as part of the top-secret Manhattan Project to build the atomic bomb. I was promoted to staff sergeant, and remained there after the war ended. One of my jobs was taking shorthand dictation from the radiology crews about the effects of the atomic bombs on Hiroshima and Nagasaki.

Next I was assigned to Operation Crossroads, working at the University of California at Berkeley, where preparations were being made to do nuclear testing in the South Pacific. We handled the credentials, lodging and travel arrangements for some 600 scientists and engineers.

I was discharged in July 1946, but stayed on the job, now as an employee of the U.S. Atomic Energy Commission.

My supervisor was Col. Stafford Warren, a physician and pioneer in nuclear medicine. When he became dean of the new medical school at UCLA, I accepted a transfer there, too, keeping a position in personnel.

Thanks to the WAC, I had a career that gave my life direction—from coast to coast!

MELBA JOHNSON
LA CANADA FLINTRIDGE, CA

MY AMAZING RIDE AS A FLIGHT NURSE

Like many World War II veterans, I thought I'd seen the last of the fighting when I came home.

After 250 missions and 25 transatlantic flights, I returned to my old job with United Air Lines. By 1950, I was back in active duty as a flight nurse, this time in Korea. When that war was over, I'd clocked another 175 air evacuation missions.

That had all begun at nursing school in San Francisco. By the time I graduated, I was fascinated with flying and had decided to become a flight attendant.

This was in the late '30s and early '40s. Few people flew then, and many of my passengers were famous. I met Eleanor Roosevelt, Olivia de Havilland and Charles Lindbergh. Once I even had a date with Cary Grant!

When World War II started, I joined the Army Air Corps so I could practice nursing and still keep flying.

We carried supplies for Patton's Third Army and flew back the wounded. There were no doctors on the evacuation flights, so we nurses had lots to do, administering pain injections, changing dressings and assuring the boys they were being sent to a military hospital. Most of them were just relieved to be getting out of a combat zone.

In 1953, I became the technical adviser for *Flight Nurse*, a Hollywood movie based on my experiences and those of the 801st Medical Air Evacuation Transport Squadron. The star, Joan Leslie (with me and actor Richard Simmons, above right), and the director, John Ford, later became godparents to my first child, Lillianne.

In 1961, Col. Barney Oldfield, Dwight Eisenhower's public information officer, asked me to meet TV host Ralph Edwards and do a public service spot for the Air Force Nurse Corps.

But it was a ruse: I ended up as the star of one of the last episodes of the early reality show *This Is Your Life*! The episode got an enormous response, probably because so many wounded veterans recognized me.

My military career put me in danger many times, but I have no regrets. I'm grateful to have been part of history.

LILLIAN KEIL COVINA, CA

SERVICE IN THE CWAC WAS A PIECE OF CAKE

May 1, 1944, was one of the most exciting days of my life. I joined the Canadian Women's Army Corps (CWAC). And it was my 18th birthday to boot!

It was a busy day, starting with a recruitment poster photo (right) taken of me cutting a cake with one candle for my first day in the Army. My sister Gladys (to my right), who had been in the CWAC for two months, was in the picture, too, along with a CWAC sergeant and the recruiting officer.

That big first day included medical exams, vaccinations, uniform issue and meeting the rest of the girls. Finally, we received our orders for Kitchener, Ontario, where we would take basic training.

We didn't get much sleep the night before we left. Not long after everyone went to bed, the fire alarm sounded.

I jumped out of bed, forgetting I was in the upper bunk, and landed hard on my knees and face. Only later did I realize I had injured my nose.

The fire was put out quickly, and we were able to go back to bed. This time, I reminded myself I was in an upper bunk.

We took the train from Winnipeg to Ontario. On the way to dinner that first day, we had to pass through a coach of young male soldiers, who greeted us with catcalls and whistles.

As our sergeant marched us back through the men's coach after dinner, the men sang, "Be kind to your web-footed friend, for that quack may be somebody's mother!" "Quack," of course, meant "CWAC."

After breakfast the next day, we were allowed to visit in the men's coach, with our sergeant and theirs as chaperones. One soldier had an accordion and another a guitar. We sang, snapped pictures and exchanged addresses.

On the third day, the train stopped at Camp Borden, Ontario, where the men would take tank training. There were promises to write and to get together on leave.

There were some tears, too. I shed my own over a soldier from Saskatchewan named Tom Hubbard. We began writing and managed to see each other twice before he went overseas and I began my training to become a CWAC secretary.

Tom and I continued to write, and I sent him packages of candy and cookies. At the USO, I made a record of our song, "I'll Get By." Tom told me later that he couldn't find a phonograph needle, so he used a toothpick. My singing wasn't the greatest, so I can only imagine how the record sounded.

Both of us were discharged in 1946. He went to college in Vancouver, where I joined him. We were married in 1947.

Tom graduated with a degree in forestry. We were blessed with two daughters and a son and enjoyed 23 wonderful years together.

JEAN BRIMS HUBBARD
WEST VANCOUVER, BC

BEHAVE, WAVE "I had a lot of fun with my maiden name, Zeman, when I was a WAVE during WWII," writes Pat Johnson of Green Valley, Arizona. "We were called seamen. In class, we had to 'sound off' with our names to the officer instructor, named Benson. So when I had a question, I said, 'Seaman Zeman, Ensign Benson.' That never failed to get a laugh."

YOUR AUNT DAISY? COME ON, BOB!

While I was with the Army Air Forces in Miami during World War II, my nephew Robert Battenfield, an Army paratrooper, was dropped somewhere in France to aid the French resistance.

He told his group that he had an aunt in the Army but didn't mention that, at age 23, I was younger than he was. Bob wrote to ask for a picture of me in uniform—specifically a cheesecake picture. This photo (above) is what my friends and I, trying to oblige, came up with.

When the picture arrived, Bob had a lot of fun passing it around. He said it was a big hit, although not all of his buddies were convinced that I was really his aunt.

DAISY DUNBAR NEW YORK, NY

ICE CREAM EASILY CROSSED CULTURES

In 1950, I was a WAC stationed at Camp Fowler in Japan. An orphanage was near our post, and often we treated the children.

Once we brought ice cream. The kids didn't know what the little wooden spoons were for, so they used chopsticks to eat it!

SHIRLEY HAERTHER
ST. PETERSBURG, FL

PAINFUL PARADE

This photo was taken on the day we took part in a parade all through St. Louis, Missouri, on Memorial Day 1953. Pictured from left are me, from Illinois; Marilyn Mann, from California; Pat Edgerly, from New Jersey; and a woman from New York whose name I don't remember.

Someone said the parade was 9 miles long, and it sure seemed like it, especially if one was marching in what we called our "old ladies shoes." We had come up from Lackland Air Force Base in Texas in early spring on our way to Scott AFB in Illinois.

We were to learn about radios, with which I had absolutely no experience. I followed the instructions to make a crystal radio set, then asked the sergeant for the wire and plug. My face turned scarlet when he explained that a plug wasn't necessary.

MARYJANE HEADLEY KEARNEY, MO

HITCHHIKERS HIT IT LUCKY

In the summer of 1944, we were three young lieutenants who had just finished flight school in Goldsboro, North Carolina. Having the whole weekend free, we decided to try our hand at hitchhiking.

Pretty soon a car stopped. The driver asked where we were going, to which we responded, "Anywhere you're going!"

The driver, a photographer, was on his way to nearby Wilson to take pictures of contestants in a beauty contest. He explained that the contest had even gained a bit of fame since the year before, when the winner was an exciting new actress named Ava Gardner.

Our hearts leaped when we turned in to the grounds of a country club and saw a bevy of beautiful women in bathing suits walking around the pool.

We were properly introduced and were asked to pose with them (I'm second from left). A South American officer joined us.

After that session, the friendly photographer had another job at a Greek wedding and said we could come along. I was fortunate enough to get one of the girls to go with me, and we had a wonderful evening of dining and dancing. Then I walked her home, kissed her good night and caught a bus back to the base.

Two months later, we were sent into combat and never saw those lovely ladies again. But we'd never forget that weekend full of wonderful surprises.

JAMES POWERS IRVINE, CA

▼ FUN PRESERVERS

There wasn't much time for playing around during basic training for the SPARs (the Coast Guard Women's Reserve) at Palm Beach, Florida, in 1944, says Betty Sherrell (right) of Campbell, California. But she and her roommate did get a moment to act a little silly!

GIVE A SAILOR A LIFT "After basic training in 1943, my buddy Art Majerus and I arranged to meet in Washington, D.C.," says Ernie Lamson of St. Paul, Minnesota. "That's me holding up Art, who was in the Coast Guard. I was an 82nd Airborne Army paratrooper. We've been friends in St. Paul since the '30s and still play golf. He introduced me to his cousin Charlene, who became my wife."

"In the winter of 1942 at Fort Richardson, Alaska, one of our Army buddies, Henry Hokenson, wouldn't get up for breakfast. So we carried him, bunk and all, into the 30-below air. He still didn't wake up! Eventually we felt sorry for him and carried him back in."

ELMER RENVALL PARK RAPIDS, MN

On the Homefront
RATIONS, RIVETS AND ROMANCE

SORE FEET AND SHY SAILORS

As I arrived at the lodge hall that Sunday in spring 1944, cars stuffed with servicemen were pulling into the parking lot in Shorewood, Wisconsin. Excited, I hurried to join the other USO hostesses. I was 19, and duty called!

Seeing the dance floor filling up with olive drab and navy blue bodies, the bandleader had us form circles for a mixer: men on the outside, ladies on the inside. On the first go-round, I found myself in the arms of a dancer who believed in the pump handle approach. By the time the music stopped, my arms were limp from flapping. Now *this* was fun!

When the band took a break, a former high school girlfriend grabbed my hand and pulled me toward the microphone. Joyce started: "Gonna take a sentimental journey…" I joined in singing alto harmony, and we swayed in unison.

At the final words, "journey home," the crowd clapped and whistled. We were tongue-tied when a sailor slapped us on the back and said, "Just like the Andrews Sisters!"

After supper, we all said our goodbyes and swapped a few addresses. It was truly a sentimental journey I'll never forget.

MARY BAER SOUTH MILWAUKEE, WI

USO FUN A photographer captured Mary Baer (seated at right, wearing a floral blouse) with the other hostesses; shy dancers lined up for a mixer (above).

FELLOW POW GAVE
MY FOLKS HOPE

"So long!" we shouted to our friend Ray. Grinning, he replied, "So long, you guys! I just wish I could take all of you along with me."

It was a cold gray day in December 1944 when Ray Kusela trudged out the gate of Stalag Luft IV in northern Poland, never to be seen by any of us again.

When Ray's bomber was shot down over Germany a year or so before, his left arm was badly wounded. The Germans knew he'd never be able to use his left hand again, and, because of that disability, he was being repatriated to the U.S.

My B-17 had been shot down on Nov. 2, 1944. But back in the States, all that my distraught parents knew was that I'd been classified as Missing in Action. Not until February 1945 were they officially notified that I was being held prisoner somewhere in German territory.

That same month, my mother read in the *Los Angeles Times* that the War Department was sponsoring meetings for relatives of prisoners of war. Ex-POWs talked to these audiences about our lives in the prison camps.

There was to be such a meeting at the Los Angeles Shrine Auditorium. My mom and dad could hardly wait.

About a week later, they anxiously took their seats in the big auditorium. Half a dozen soldiers and sailors, all ex-POWs, sat on the stage. Among them was Ray Kusela.

After a few brief speeches, the officer in charge announced, "The men will now go down into the audience to look at any photos you brought along. Some of them may be recognized."

The audience crowded forward, extending photos of their missing sweethearts, husbands and sons. Later, Dad told me what happened next:

"Your mother and I had been feeling really bad since we got the telegram that you were missing. But those boys on that stage gave us hope.

"I watched this one fellow pushing his way through the crowd, looking at the pictures—hundreds of them—held out to him. He just shook his head and kept saying, 'No. No. No.'

"By the time he got to where your mother and I were, I began to feel dejected again. But I held out your picture, and that kid's face lit up with a great big grin and he said, 'Hey, that's Bill!'"

Dad said he had to hold back a sob when he asked, "Is he OK?"

"He's fine," Ray assured them.

Mom and Dad cried together on their way home that night, hearing over and over again those wonderful words: He's fine.

I will be forever beholden to Ray Kusela of Bremerton, Washington, someone I knew for only a few weeks. He did me and my family the greatest favor of any man I've ever known.
BILL LIVINGSTONE
SANTA BARBARA, CA

FOREVER GRATEFUL Bill Livingstone (top left as a POW in 1944) waited to celebrate his liberation, as these troops from a Japanese camp did (below).

RED CROSS GREETERS SERVED WITH A SMILE

While my husband, Bill, was fighting his way across Europe in 1944, I was part of a Red Cross welcoming committee greeting wounded soldiers who'd been shipped home.

Our job was to hand out little treats and give the boys a heartfelt welcome home. Most important of all, we were instructed to smile.

Single file, we followed our military escort to the lowest deck of the ship, where the wounded lay on their litters. We heard, "Hey, it's girls!" as we distributed candy and comic books.

Often, though, we'd come to a bunk where a young soldier lay silently, with tears trickling down his cheeks. He'd turn his head away as we put a candy bar beside him.

In April 1946, I traveled to Germany to join my husband. At the train station (below), I was greeted by a Red Cross volunteer.

PEGGY DOWNEY-KNOWLTON
ARLINGTON, VA

I WAS A TEENAGE "WELDERETTE"

In 1944, I had just graduated from high school and was working in a bakery. That's when I saw an ad placed by Kaiser Shipyard offering free train fare to Vancouver, Washington, where a job and a room in a dormitory awaited.

Ready for adventure, I signed up, packed my clothes and guitar and waved goodbye to South Dakota. In Vancouver, a bus took me to my new home, where I roomed with a girl named Trudy from Missouri, who remained a good friend. Our dorms had housemothers whom we came to love. The boys had their own dorms, but we got together in the lounges after work and had a great time singing and playing our instruments.

I started as a pipe welder, earning between $2 and $3 an hour—big wages at the time. We wore welder hoods, goggles, leather gloves, jackets and pants. Often we had to weld pipes together in the ships' bathrooms, in spaces so small our lead man had to push us in and pull us out. We also had to take tests to make sure our welds didn't leak. I remember asking my foreman if I passed. He said, "You had a weld on there that wouldn't leak for 50 years," so I was happy.

Sometimes celebrities came to launch a ship when it was finished. I saw both Gypsy Rose Lee and Cesar Romero.

The day the war was over, a group of us got into a car and drove to Portland, Oregon, to watch the ships come in. What a thrill! I wish now I had saved my welder's leathers and hood. (I did save the photo above—I'm the silly one in the middle.)
NORMA AMAN JERKE KALAMAZOO, MI

PARACHUTE TO THE RESCUE

In college during WWII, I met Howard Van Loon, a fellow student who shared my call to ministry. We fell in love and were planning a postwar wedding. But, like other brides-to-be, I had a problem. During the war, the textile industry had focused on other needs, so wedding gowns were hard to come by.

That's when my brother David, an Air Force pilot who'd flown in the South Pacific, offered me his wartime trophy—a white silk parachute. My mother ripped it apart and was able to salvage much of the beautiful material for my gown (below).

Because the scarcity of wedding dresses continued, various friends were grateful for the use of my dress for their own grand celebrations. Then, in the late 1940s, the parachute gown underwent yet another transformation.

At a conference, I heard a speaker talk about her ministry on the island of Borneo, where a wedding dress in hand was required when a young man proposed marriage. When I asked if there was a need for such a garment, she answered with an enthusiastic yes! So the precious silk was resurrected for its loving return to the South Pacific.

JODIE BRUNNER VAN LOON PASADENA, CA

GLORIOUS DAY! Hearing of Japan's surrender on Aug. 15, 1945, Ruth Sippel of West Hills, California (in the plaid dress), and her friends celebrated the end of the war by staging an impromptu sidewalk parade in Roseland, Illinois, complete with decorated bikes and wagons. Even pets helped welcome the long-awaited return of peace.

A BONDING EXPERIENCE "My Grandmother Hazel was buying war bonds at one of the tank-replica sales stands that were set up throughout the city," writes Gail Bird of Arvada, Colorado. "My brother Jack and I are wearing play combat helmets."

SWEATER GIRLS "In 1943, most of our male co-workers at Metropolitan Life Insurance Co., on 23rd Street in New York City, had been drafted to fight for our freedom," says Grace Kreusser Lavin of Bridgewater, New Jersey. "Known as Henderson's Girls in Department 929, we were sending newsletters to the company's servicemen to keep them up on happenings around the office. As a special Valentine's Day surprise, we decided to get creative and send them this photo from the 929 Sweater Girls. That's me posed at top left."

The American Dream

OUR AMERICAN MOMENT

We watched as the trunk carrying all of our belongings descended to the New York City dock below. On its side were written my last name and first initial, along with "Liverpool to New York."

It was June of 1957, and we had just crossed the Atlantic after leaving our home in Belfast, Ireland. We sailed on the ocean liner *HMS Britannic* from England's coast.

It had taken us two years of work and saving to arrive at this point in our lives. We were ultimately headed for Chicago, where I planned to continue my theological education. I told my wife, Catherine, to wait by the trunk with our daughter, Sharon, while I went to see what to do next.

Suddenly, a thin man approached me, calling me by first name and asking if I was on my way to a certain theological school in Chicago.

I soon learned the man was a nephew of an elderly couple I had met briefly before leaving Ireland. They'd asked him to meet us at the dock.

We received a hearty welcome at the man's home, including hot meals and comfortable beds. Over the weekend, we visited the top of the Empire State Building. We were amazed to see New York City and its environs spread out below. Here was America, in all of its grandeur and success.

On Monday, we boarded a Greyhound to Chicago. Such kindness is what makes America great.
WALLACE BELL OCEANSIDE, CA

NEW HOME Catherine and Wallace Bell, on the *HMS Britannic* (left) and with children Paul and Sharon (above) in Vaughn, Washington, six years after they came to the U.S.

PATRIOTIC PIPER
She was born in Scotland, but Henrietta Moore (here in 1940) was red, white and true-blue.

MOM, THE FEISTY FOREIGN PATRIOT

You might wonder how a foreigner can also be a patriot, but it's easy. My mother, Henrietta, was one. After growing up in Scotland and moving to America, she fell in love with her adopted country and became an honest-to-goodness patriot.

We lived in Chicago, and during World War II, Mom did things that many people born in this country never even thought of doing.

Every Saturday during summer, before we could play baseball, my brother Al and I had to rake the white stones at the memorial built on our block to honor neighborhood men who'd died for their country. Meanwhile, Mom climbed a ladder to polish the brass nameplates listing the fallen while our baby brother watched from his buggy.

The neighbors made a big mistake when they appointed Mom as air raid warden. She acquired a hard hat, armband, flashlight and baton—but most of all, she acquired power. When Mom knocked on someone's door and said "Lights out," she meant it.

Al and I came home from school for lunch every day, and we couldn't go back to school until we'd heard Kate Smith sing a patriotic song on the radio.

What more could Mom do for her country? The answer was the USO. When it asked for donations of books for servicemen, Mom was ready. Al and I were sorry she heard this on the radio, because the drop-off point downtown was a long way from our home. But that didn't stop my mother.

Dad was an avid reader, so our garage was full of books. Mom loaded Al and me with stacks of paperbacks, and we all boarded the bus. Al and I went to the back of the bus, embarrassed to be toting all this stuff.

Mom, also carrying a stack of books, sat up front with our baby brother. Then she embarrassed us further by trying to give up her seat when a soldier stepped on. "God bless you," he said, telling her to please stay in her seat.

An hour and a half later, we arrived at the USO with the books. After Mom had talked to a lot of servicemen and cheered them up, we started for home.

A few weeks later, she put a star in our front window. This was supposed to mean you had a son or daughter in the service. We reminded Mom she didn't have anyone in the service. She said, "But I do have a nephew." Mom had her own set of rules.

Everyone knew she didn't have a child old enough for the military, but no one had the guts to say anything. Though only 4-foot-11, this Scottish lass would turn into a tigress if her patriotism were questioned.

Years later, Mom was so proud to see both her sons go into the service—me in the Navy and Al in the Army. This time, two stars went up in our window. I don't know where Mom found them—the war was over, and they hadn't been made for some time.

Al and I have often been accused of being flag wavers, but with a mother like ours, how could we turn out any other way?

In her 66 years in the U.S., Mom never took her rights for granted—she figured she had to earn them. And there were no foreigners in the America she knew. Everyone had an equal share of freedom.

I've had the privilege of carrying the American flag in parades and presentations for many years. Whenever I carry it today, the patriotism Mom instilled in me makes me the proudest man alive.

ERWIN MOORE GARDEN GROVE, CA

GOD BLESS AMERICA

In February 1945, my parents, my brother and I had been confined in the Santo Tomas internment camp near Manila, in the Philippines, for three years after the Japanese took over the island.

I was 7 when I told my mother about the shadow of a huge bird I had seen going across the hot, dry grounds of the camp a week before. She told me not to say anything about what I had seen.

It was not a bird, of course, but a low-flying American airplane.

For some time, the Filipinos outside our fence had been singing "God Bless America" as their way of letting us know that American troops were coming soon to liberate us.

On a warm tropical night soon after, the tanks of the 1st

NICE TO BE HOME The author, then Betty Lou Cushing, is pictured at right with her brother, Charles Jr., in 1941, and in America (above) with her parents, Mercedes and Charlie, and other family members.

Cavalry Division and a flying column of American soldiers crashed through the gates of the internment camp, overpowered the guards and liberated us.

For the first time, we could leave our rooms at night. The next morning, the American soldiers shared their rations with internees, many of whom were near starvation.

There had been a lot of bombing around Manila the nights before our liberation. I recall my father telling us, "Look, there where the sky is red. That's

a rocket, and there are bombs."

"The rockets' red glare, the bombs bursting in air," someone suddenly said. People had tears in their eyes. I didn't understand the words then. Patriotic songs were forbidden in the camp.

When all of us arrived back in America, I was able to go to school, learning to read and write and sing.

Now I love to sing, and "God Bless America" is my favorite song. Every time we sing it in my church choir, I still get a thrill.

BETTY SONDERMAN SONORA, CA

"CHEESE, PLEASE"

It was 1950. I was newly arrived from Germany and on my way across the U.S. to Los Angeles by bus. We stopped at a depot for a break, and I was hungry. I had taken English in high school in Berlin and prided myself on speaking the language reasonably well. But this lunch counter menu had me baffled.

Hot dogs? Chili dogs? I couldn't imagine what a heated or "chilled" dog could be.

Finally, I came across one simple entry: "Cheese sandwich." When a waitress in a starched uniform asked for my order, I said, "A cheese sandwich, please."

"Do you want…?" The end of her question was unintelligible. Still, I nodded "yes" to each inquiry. When she brought my order, it turned out to be American cheese on white bread with mayonnaise and lettuce.

After a few bites, I thought it was pretty good. And the potato chips that came with it were wonderful. American food was also reasonably priced. The $50 my sponsor had advanced me would be more than sufficient to see me across this big country.

We rode through Pennsylvania, where the countryside reminded me of Germany. Soon it was time for lunch. Again, the bus station menu was impossible for me to understand. So when another waitress asked for my order, I said, "A cheese sandwich, please."

This version, Swiss on rye with caraway seeds, was even more delightful than the last.

The next morning at breakfast, a fellow passenger sat down beside me. An elderly lady, she correctly assumed I was new to this country. I was enthralled to be having my first real English conversation. I told the woman how I'd applied for my visa in 1948 and that it had been two long years before I was able to sail to America.

I struggled, with my limited English, to tell her the stories of my youth: of dodging bombs during air raids, riding atop boxcars and foraging for food for myself and my starving sisters.

"Well, have a safe trip," the woman said. "I hope you will find all you are seeking and more." As she left, she picked up my bill and paid it. With tears in my eyes, I thanked her.

What a wonderful country that I will soon be able to call

home, I thought. Having gained confidence, I was sure I would be able to talk more intelligently with the next waitress.

And so it continued, cheese sandwich after cheese sandwich, no two exactly alike, but all of them tasty. To a war victim who'd often gone hungry, the diversity of this one sandwich was simply astounding. And I was very grateful for the chance to be in a country where a simple cheese sandwich could become an unforgettable adventure.

ANNEMARIE REUTER SCHOMAKER
RAMONA, CA

COUPLE OF GOOD CITIZENS

My mom and I lived with Grandma Mollie, Grandpa Jacob, Aunt Ethel and Uncle Bernard when I started kindergarten in the late '30s. Going to school was scary for me, but Grandma held my hand, walked with me each day and eased my fears.

Grandma Mollie (beside me at left) was born in Odessa, Ukraine, and had very limited schooling. She loved her adopted country, though, and decided to become a citizen. She enrolled in a course that met once a week from 6 to 8 p.m. By then I was 9, old enough to walk Grandma to school.

I stayed in the class the entire two hours and helped Grandma with her English, and the teacher let me help anyone else who needed it. It was fun!

After several months, Grandma and her classmates received their citizenship certificates. There was a party, and our whole family was invited. We were all proud of Grandma Mollie.

I was proud of myself, too. I'd helped Grandma over some of the rough spots, just as she did years before when I was in kindergarten. After all, one good turn deserves another.

RHODA FISHER BOYNTON BEACH, FL

Reader Favorites

CANDID COURAGE Before being evacuated to a hospital in the U.K., an injured Lt. James Tate (far right) refused to leave behind this picture of his wife, Ellen.

LOST AND FOUND

We walked slowly through the wet grass, our eyes searching for the subtlest sign of the enemy. I wondered why our artillery wasn't throwing shells when we knew they were there that early morning in Normandy.

Suddenly, the percussive rattle of machine-gun fire broke the quiet. We instinctively hit the ground, barely sheltered from the shots by a low stone wall a few feet ahead.

My radioman called the company commander to report as I summoned two soldiers to help me locate and knock out the relentless machine gun.

While I crouched on one knee to talk to my guys, I heard an explosion—and the next thing I remember I was on my back, trying to breathe.

"Lieutenant! Lieutenant! You've been hit!" the radioman shouted over the din.

Two medics strapped me to a stretcher and took me to an aid station. A doc slapped a bandage on my bloody knee. Then the medics drove me to a nearby field hospital.

They carried me into a crowded tent where dozens of wounded soldiers were lined up on the ground.

I watched the nurses dispense shots before things went black. When I woke up, I was lying on a cot wearing nothing but my dog tags and a blanket.

"Wake up, Lieutenant!" a nurse shouted. "You've got to get on a plane—you're flying to a hospital in England!"

I panicked. All my worldly possessions lay in a mountainous heap of equipment. I could replace everything except the photo of my new bride, Ellen, which I always carried with me.

"I'm not going until I get my wife's picture," I said. "It's inside the gas mask cover you took away from me."

I knew the nurse could make me go, but instead she said, "OK, I'll see if I can find it," then ran out to search through the piles. Time stood still until she finally came back running breathlessly into our tent.

"I've got it!" she shouted, waving the picture in her upraised hand. How she found it I'll never know, but I'm sure glad she did. That photograph comforted me through tough times. And for seven decades afterward, it has sat on my bedside table.

JAMES TATE MOUNT PLEASANT, SC

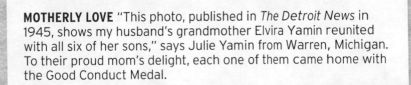

MOTHERLY LOVE "This photo, published in *The Detroit News* in 1945, shows my husband's grandmother Elvira Yamin reunited with all six of her sons," says Julie Yamin from Warren, Michigan. To their proud mom's delight, each one of them came home with the Good Conduct Medal.

CAREFREE COURTIN' "This is my mother and father, Rosemary Ellen O'Donnell and Austin G. Reiman, during their dating period in the early '40s," writes Jody Reiman Dutt of Bethlehem, Pennsylvania. "Sundays were spent differently before the attack on Pearl Harbor, shortly after which my father enlisted. For him, this particular Sunday was filled with memories of going to Central Park in Bethlehem, winning his best girl a great big teddy bear, and then taking pictures for the scrapbook."

CHAPTER 4

True Romance

A candid look at romance is apt to make any heart skip a beat. From that memorable first date to the wedding day, stories of young love abound in the pages of *Reminisce* magazine. It's nearly impossible to resist these lighthearted tales of first encounters that led to happily ever after.

Young Love

AT FIRST, LOVE FLEW SOLO

Even though Darlene and I were high school classmates in Harlan, Iowa, we barely knew each other. I didn't date back then, as I spent most of my time happily building model airplanes and taking flying lessons.

One day, as I was coming back to school after lunch, I bumped into Darlene. She struck up a conversation, and I found it easy to talk with her. The memory of that experience stayed with me even after we graduated and went our separate ways.

Fast-forward three years to the spring of 1952. I was hospitalized in Omaha, Nebraska, because of back surgery when who should walk into my room but Darlene! She was a student nurse. Darlene visited me almost every day after that. Just as we had that day in high school years before, we enjoyed very pleasant conversations. I even promised that I would give her an airplane ride one day.

When I recovered from surgery and left Omaha, I couldn't stop thinking about Darlene. So the next February, while I was in Tulsa, Oklahoma, and attending the Spartan School of Aeronautics, I decided to take matters into my own hands. After all, I certainly couldn't count on fate to keep bringing the two of us together.

I sent Darlene a valentine, and she responded with a letter—as well as a reminder that I still owed her an airplane ride.

I made good on my promise. One year after that hospital stay in Omaha, I flew to Harlan for my first date with Darlene. And, yes, I did give her an airplane ride—her first one, in fact.

Darlene and I got engaged on our fifth date and married on Sept. 16, 1953. Two daughters and five grandchildren later, I'm so glad we finally got on the same flight path!

DWIGHT TAYLOR ST. CHARLES, MO

FLYING HIGH Darlene Klitgaard (at right) reconnected with classmate Dwight Taylor in 1952. A year later, he flew to see her for their first date (at far right). Today, life is still an adventure for the pair (above).

REUNITED The author and Edna (left) are pictured in 1949 after a misunderstanding. Their wedding photo includes Birney's father, Paul, and mother, Marie.

A CURE FOR LOVESICKNESS

When I was a junior in medical school, I needed to make my first attempt at drawing blood from a patient. A young nurse accompanied me to the bedside with a tray that held a tourniquet, syringe and sponge.

After I successfully drew a sample, my efficient helper whisked the paraphernalia away. I called out to her, "Thank you, Miss—er—uhm."

"Baird," she called back.

A few minutes later, I walked over to the nurses station on the pretext of leaving the lab slips but actually to get a look at her name tag. "Miss Edna Baird." I also took a look at her left hand. No ring. OK! She would probably be living in the nurses residence across the street from the medical school.

I called her that night. Yes, she would love to go to a movie with me Friday night. So we went. And fell in love—or at least I did. We dated every Friday night for the next three months. I remember sitting on a rather drafty Chicago red rattler headed downtown to the Loop to see a movie when the thought hit me like a sledgehammer: *This is the girl I'm going to marry!* I proposed

to her that night, she said yes, and we lived happily ever after. Right? Sorry—not on your tintype, as we used to say back then.

A few weeks later, I called the nurses residence and asked to speak with Miss Baird.

"Oh, I'm sorry, sir. She's gone."

"OK, will you ask her to call me when she gets in? She knows the number."

"No, sir. I mean she's really gone. She moved out this afternoon."

I was stunned. All those months of dates and fraternity parties and smooching in the frat living room with the lights out meant nothing to her? She was the girl I was going to marry! Or was she?

When my head cleared, I called her roommate, Martha. Edna had taken a job in New Mexico. And, no, Martha didn't have an address. Needless to say, it was one miserable summer.

I went back to school in October to begin my senior year. After the 8 o'clock lecture, I reported to the surgery ward. And there was Miss Edna Baird.

She took a look around—checking to see if the head nurse was in earshot, no doubt—and then rushed up to me and took both my hands in hers.

"Birney! Why didn't you write?"

"Write? How could I? I didn't have a clue to where you were!"

Unfeigned dismay crossed her face and she said sadly, "But I left you a note."

We finally sorted it out. She had gotten a call from a friend who was spending her summer vacation as a counselor at a Girl Scout camp near Albuquerque, and the camp needed a nurse immediately.

After nobody answered at my fraternity house, Edna wrote me a note giving me her new address and imploring me to write. She left it with a patient I had been working with for weeks and was scheduled to see the next day.

I remembered the man…and the fact that he'd been transferred to another ward the day Edna disappeared. What happened to that note? Edna and I never found out.

We made a date for that night and made up for lost time. I asked her to marry me, and she said yes.

We were married for 52 years. I'm sorry to say that she's gone now to her heavenly home, where someday she'll take my hands in hers and say, "Birney!"

BIRNEY DIBBLE EAU CLAIRE, WI

A GLANCE AND A WINK

In 1942, while riding the bus from Coeymans High School to my home in Selkirk, New York, I spotted a great-looking girl crossing the Ravena High School yard. I saw her glance in my direction and quickly winked at her. She immediately winked back. I eventually found out her name was Doris and got up the nerve to ask for a date.

When I went to pick her up at her family's dairy farm in nearby Coeymans Hollow, Doris was about to herd the cows into the barn. It didn't matter that she had a date; it was her duty. I pitched in and helped her complete the chore, and we went on to a school dance.

I joined the Navy after my graduation, and when I came home on leave in 1944, we had this photo taken, showing just how strong this farm girl was. We were married in 1946, and I often think back on how quickly I was smitten with a farm girl I first saw at a glance.

PETE HOFFMAN RIO VISTA, CA

PEDALING VICTORY CORN

My school friend Clarence Ellingham and I planted a victory garden of corn during World War II. Our garden was different from most, as it was 12 miles from our Chicago neighborhood, in Midlothian, Illinois, where Clarence's parents had a lot.

Our only transportation was Clarence's bicycle (above). I rode on the crossbar of the handlebars, carrying our garden tools.

A man who lived near the garden kindly let us store our tools and let us use his hose and water. We were happy to share our crop when the corn was ripe.

We had made several trips to the garden when Clarence's mom, Leona, made a cushion for me that she attached to the crossbar of the bike.

I'm happy to say that years later, this thoughtful and kind lady became my mother-in-law.

MARGARET CRESS ELLINGHAM LAKE HAVASU CITY, AZ

LOVE GOT A FIGHTING CHANCE

On a Saturday afternoon in 1939, my college teammates and I had won our second football game. Saturday evening was date night for members of my fraternity, but I used the time for homework.

I was working on a research paper when I was interrupted by two teammates. We chatted about the afternoon's victory, and they mentioned that they were dating two girls from one of the sororities. They were seeking a substitute date for a third gal whose beau had to work.

When I declined because of my research paper, my friends' demeanor soon changed. Both were over 6 feet tall and well more than 200 pounds of muscle.

I could see their change in countenance and noticed that their hands were becoming fists. With resignation, I agreed to join the group at the dance.

I must admit that my date, Carol, and I enjoyed the evening. We also discovered that we were in the same Physics 201 class. We soon were meeting every day after class, and it wasn't long before our acquaintance grew to friendship, and just around the corner, we found love.

I failed to keep in touch with the two 6-footers, but I thank them every day for that moment when their hands turned to fists. That's what led to a life with a woman whose devotion embodied sincere compassion and love.

RICHARD ROWE KAMUELA, HI

PHOTOGRAPHIC COUPLE "My parents, Marjorie and Norman Humphrey, were always going on fun outings during their dating years, 1936-'40," writes Mary Ann Humphrey-Keever of Portland, Oregon. "They loved using their Kodak box cameras. This 1938 photo shows them, cameras in hand. The photo was colored from black and white film for $3.34. I have their cameras, and as far as I know, they still work."

REMEMBER DANCE CARDS?

"My husband, Ted, and I had our first real date on Valentine's Day 1953, when we went to a sock hop after a basketball game," writes Charlotte Bender of Elyria, Ohio. "Back then, girls attending a formal dance hung a dance card around the wrist. When opened, the card revealed blank lines for the names of up to 20 men. Of course, my dance card always had only one name–'Ted'–splashed across all the lines. The two of us went to quite a few dances at Mount Union College in Alliance, Ohio, and I saved a number of my dance cards. In December 1954, we became officially engaged. The next April, we were married in Texas. Ted now 'filled my dance card' every day!"

WIFE IN THE WINDOW "My dad, Richard Garber, was stationed near Denver with the Army Air Corps, and Mom, then Grace Grager (far left), worked for the May Co., which made military uniforms," writes Linda Miller of Melbourne, Florida. "As a promotion, the company selected Mom and her friend Fern Wentland to work in a display window in downtown Denver. Dad waited one night for her to come out of the store and invited her to a dinner, and the rest is history. They were married in Denver in September 1943, just months after meeting. Mom and Dad enjoyed 57 years of marriage and always loved telling their story."

A REAL SWEETHEART "During their courting days, my dad, Melvin Johnson, would bring my mother, Mabel Fossen, the chocolate bars that she enjoyed," says Doris Engebretson of Fargo, North Dakota. "This 1927 photo shows Mom with her cache of Hersheys and Mr. Goodbars, presented to her on a Sunday afternoon date."

SANTA'S WISH When Maryann Fabbri sat on Santa's lap in 1953 in Cleveland, Ohio, she had no idea that the man behind the beard would eventually ask her out and become her husband!

To Have and to Hold

UNFORGETTABLE MOMENTS OF MATRIMONY

ALASKANS WED ON TV IN NEW YORK

I came to Ketchikan, Alaska, to visit relatives in early 1951. The small town, accessible only by steamship or aircraft, had so few young ladies in the workforce that someone actually approached me on the street about a job. Before long, I was working for the Army Signal Corps' Alaska Communication System.

The Army fellows introduced me to Joe, one of their fishing buddies, and we began dating. We hiked up mountains and over trails, fished for king salmon and hunted for black-tailed deer. By the spring of '52, we knew we were in love.

Our friends said we should try to get on CBS' *Bride and Groom* TV show. We wrote in and soon got word that we'd been selected!

We later learned that 75,000 couples had applied.

On Dec. 19, 1952, we started the drive to New York, with Joe's mother as chaperone. We nearly wore out a pair of tire chains just getting through Nevada.

Arriving in New York City, we were astonished by the bright twinkling lights. It was quite an experience for small-town kids like Joe and me. His mom and I were giddy with delight as we drove through the city.

We stayed at a private home in New Jersey and went back and forth to the *Bride and Groom* set in New York to "practice." Two marriages took place during each half-hour show, before a live audience of about 35. The show was in black and white, but we were surprised that the appliances were yellow—so

they wouldn't glare on TV. All of us, even Joe, were adorned with makeup for the same reason.

Our ceremony took place on New Year's Eve. A young fellow from my Alaska office was home in Pennsylvania on leave, so he was Joe's best man. My mother-in-law gave me an old lace veil, a new blue garter and a borrowed diamond pin, so I had something old, new, borrowed and blue. My beautiful satin wedding gown was provided by the show.

Joe's tuxedo never arrived, so he was married in his blue suit. We'd bought our own rings, but the show provided a set, too. Mine was set with three Keepsake diamonds.

After the wedding, the gown was returned to the show, and we left on a five-day, all-expenses-paid honeymoon at Virginia Beach.

From Virginia Beach, we drove on through Florida, along the Gulf Coast, west to California and then up to Washington and Alaska. It was the trip of a lifetime. We kept a daily diary and still love to read it every few years.

Joe's mom visited family in Massachusetts before returning home. She was able to see herself on TV when our wedding aired later on the West Coast.

My parents went to Seattle to see it, as TV wasn't available yet in Portland, Oregon. A friend in Denver said she was about to plug in her vacuum cleaner when she heard our names and looked up to see us on TV!

Bride and Groom provided a wonderful send-off for a young couple just getting started.

BARBARA HASSELL KETCHIKAN, AK

THE HAPPY COUPLE
Barbara and Joe Hassell were selected from about 75,000 couples to be married on CBS' *Bride and Groom* TV show in 1952.

WINTER WEDDING The author (above with bridal party and at right with Dad) learned during the blizzard of '47 why most marry in summer.

BLIZZARD OF OBSTACLES COULDN'T STOP WEDDING

The East Coast blizzard on Dec. 26, 1947, was particularly memorable because my wedding was the next day!

Friday, Dec. 26, dawned gray and dismal in Passaic, New Jersey. It was snowing when Mr. Wasdyke picked me up to work at the telephone company.

By late morning, supervisors allowed employees to go home. Unfortunately, my bridesmaid Carolyn and I were not among them. When the office closed at 5, we hopped into Mr. Wasdyke's car for the trip home. By then, the snow was 18 inches deep. We made it home 2 hours late, and my mother was frantic.

The baker wanted to know whether he should go ahead with the cake, and my maid of honor and another bridesmaid called to say they couldn't make the rehearsal, which the priest had canceled anyway.

All beauty shops closed, so I set hair for Carolyn, my mother, sister and myself. I didn't go to bed until after midnight.

The next morning, the sky was clear and the snow glistened. As was tradition in our church, my fiancé, Al, and I attended Mass that morning. Afterward, Al walked to his aunt's house to dig out his father's car and retrieve his wedding clothes.

Al then walked back to the church. An oil truck offered him a lift, and when the trucker learned Al was headed to a wedding, he barked, "What idiot would get married today?"

Back home, Mother was in a state of frenzy. The telephone rang unceasingly with inquiries about the wedding. Most disturbing was a call from the photographer, who said he couldn't get there. The baker also called to say the cake couldn't be delivered, and Carolyn's bridesmaid's dress was 20 miles away. Luckily, her farmer boyfriend attached a plow to his tractor and delivered the dress.

A dear uncle fought the immense snowdrifts to pick up our wedding cake. Then the photographer showed up. He told me he'd expected all kinds of verbal abuse when he canceled, but he said I was so sweet and understanding that he just couldn't let me down.

At 5 p.m., after something of a delay to allow for late arrivals, the wedding proceeded. None of my attendants had ever been in a wedding, but they marched down the aisle perfectly. Dad and I followed, too tired to be nervous.

Fortunately, our caterers were ladies from the parish who lived close by. They prepared a magnificent Hungarian wedding feast in the church kitchen.

Winter wasn't popular for weddings, and this was the first December wedding any of our guests had attended. Later, they told us it was breathtaking. I'd have to agree that it was—in more ways than one!

CLAIRE SIKLOSI CINCINNATI, OH

HONEYMOON LESS THAN PICTURE-PERFECT

Our wedding on May 31, 1952, was beautiful. The next day, my husband, George, and I left for Daytona Beach, Florida.

After three days of rain and detours, we arrived in Daytona Beach late. George had to wake up the motel manager to get our key. I felt as though we had arrived in a honeymoon paradise.

The next morning, I awoke before George and, having seen a store across the street, decided to surprise him with a home-cooked breakfast. To my chagrin, when I awoke him with a cheery "Good morning, breakfast is ready," he responded, "Oh, no! The manager told me that if we didn't use the kitchen, he wouldn't charge us for it." After breakfast, he went down to the office to pay a hefty $9 fee.

Three evenings later, George was sitting in the car listening to a championship fight. The manager saw him and offered the use of a plastic radio so he could listen to the fight inside the bungalow.

The following day, I pulled out the table when making lunch, and the radio smashed onto the floor. George went to pay another pricey visit to the manager.

The last evening there, George backed the car into the parking space and pulled forward to straighten it out. The bumper caught a sprinkler and pulled it from the entire system. Water shot into the air like a fountain!

George was told he'd have to talk with the owner, but we needed to leave. We arrived home with $8, sure we were going to have to pay for a sprinkler system.

In the mail we found a notice that George had been accepted into the typographical union, which meant he had to leave his job. A few weeks later, I learned I was pregnant. We were thankful we never heard from the hotel again—and I'm sure the hotel people felt the same about us!

JOAN KNOPF DELAND, FL

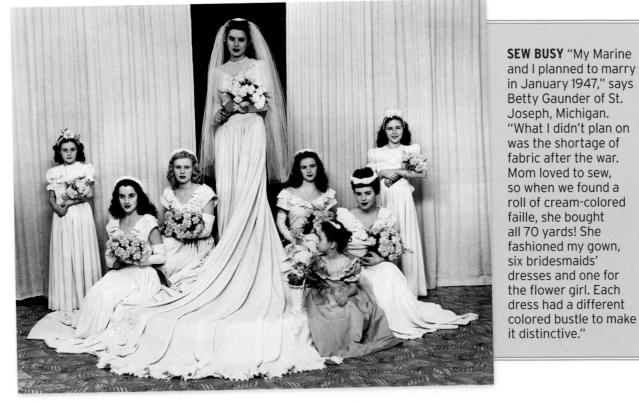

SEW BUSY "My Marine and I planned to marry in January 1947," says Betty Gaunder of St. Joseph, Michigan. "What I didn't plan on was the shortage of fabric after the war. Mom loved to sew, so when we found a roll of cream-colored faille, she bought all 70 yards! She fashioned my gown, six bridesmaids' dresses and one for the flower girl. Each dress had a different colored bustle to make it distinctive."

BEWARE OF BIG-CITY WAYS

My wife, Lily, and I were newlyweds in 1968. She was a Chinese resident of Hong Kong and in the United States for the first time, and I had just finished a tour in Vietnam.

Lily had lived all her life in a big city and was astounded by how friendly the people were in my small hometown of Knoxville, Iowa. She couldn't stop talking about it.

I tried to tell Lily that it wasn't fair to compare small-town residents with those in the big city, but she remained unconvinced.

In fact, when we arrived in Chicago for our honeymoon, she scoffed when I warned her not to expect the same warmth and kindness she enjoyed back in Knoxville.

We went out to dinner on our first night and struck up a conversation with a middle-aged couple who had just finished their meal at the next table. When they learned that we were newlyweds and that Lily was in the country for the first time, the couple kept us company during our meal.

Then they clandestinely paid our check and took us nightclubbing for the rest of the evening. They wouldn't let us pay for anything.

After the couple dropped us off at our hotel, Lily drily asked me, "When do I get to meet the unfriendly Americans in Chicago?"

I was never more proud of my country than I was that night.

LARRY STANGL PITTSBURG, CA

▲ TOP HATS AND TAILS

"My husband, Willie Lowther (far left), was best man at the wedding of his brother, Augustus, on April 23, 1943, at Bethany Baptist Church on Market Street in Newark, New Jersey," writes Hastie Lowther of New York, New York. "The bride, Pearl, who still lives in New Jersey, remembers: 'It was a great day. So many relatives and friends attended. In those days, money or no money, weddings were always fashionable.'"

▲ HONEYMOON CABIN

Back in 1954, when Tom and Joan Bare of Hatboro, Pennsylvania, were on their honeymoon at Niagara Falls, tiny tourist cabins like this one were what travelers stayed in before motels took over the landscape. The modest doorway takes up nearly half of the cabin's front wall!

▲ TUPPERWARE WAS TOPS

"In June 1962, my friend Doris Friis of Yucaipa, California, hosted a bridal shower for my daughter Robyn, who is seen entering the room wearing the tissue-paper dress that was fashioned for her," writes Geneva Houghton of Hemet. "The following Aug. 3, she became Mrs. David Looy. They still use the Tupperware gifts."

◄ QUARTER-TON OF SWEETNESS

"My parents ordered this beautiful 500-pound cake when my husband, Gene, and I were married, on May 8, 1954," says LaVerne Wesolowski of Milwaukee, Wisconsin. "The cake was shipped in sections, and the Italian baker finished decorating it on-site."

Happily Ever After
TRYING TIMES LED TO GREAT MEMORIES

NEWLYWEDS FOUND OBSERVATORY JOB A BLESSING

We were just-married kids from Chariton County, Missouri, striking out to find work and some relief from the Depression in 1936.

Getting to California was an adventure in itself for Roy and me. Our old car was a two-seater with a rumble seat. We pulled a small trailer behind us containing our trunk and a few belongings.

When we stopped for the night, we left Roy's good gloves in the back of the car, and our trunk in the trailer. Sometime during the night, we heard the car horn, so Roy jumped up and ran for the car.

The thieves escaped with the gloves, and we found the trunk pulled

halfway out of the trailer. If the thieves had taken the trunk, we would have had nothing but the clothes on our backs!

When we finally got to California, we were surprised to find fresh vegetables in January and the climate warm and mild. Back home, people were struggling with the challenges of a typical Missouri winter.

Roy's brother, Buck, and his wife and two young sons also came to California with us. Both brothers were able to sign on with a construction crew working on the two famed Mount Palomar telescopes.

The small cabin we all shared was made of rough native lumber. There was a monkey stove at one end of the cabin with an oven only big enough for a pan of biscuits.

At night, bobcats and mountain lions growled back and forth, so we tried to avoid nighttime trips to the outhouse.

We played cards or had water fights at the nearby water hydrant. Some evenings, Buck played his fiddle. We were definitely still kids.

Although we hardly had a dime, those were wonderful months. Not even the Depression could dampen our enthusiasm. We were two farm kids from Marceline, Missouri, who were in love.

FLORENCE LINEBAUGH
MARCELINE, MO

YOUNG LOVE After Florence and Roy Linebaugh (above in 1935) were married, they moved to California, where Roy helped build Mount Palomar's observatory (right). Below, the fun-loving couple are outside the tiny cabin they shared with Roy's brother's family.

AW, SHUCKS!
Dorothea Wolfe showed her future in-laws that a city girl can shuck corn with the best of them. Her fiancé, Jim, is on the left.

CITY GIRL PASSES MUSTER

My fiancé, Jim, took me back to the farm to meet his folks in February 1941. They'd already told him, "That city girl you're engaged to won't know anything about the farm."

So, of course, on the first night I was taken out to the barn to help with the milking. "Try it," Jim's mother said as I was provided with a milking stool.

They all stood around and smiled, expecting nothing to happen. But our folks had taken my brother, Al, and me to a farm every summer when we were kids, and I had learned how to milk a cow.

Swoosh, swoosh, swoosh went the milk as I filled the pail. I passed that test.

I faced another the next morning when Jim asked if I wanted to help shuck corn. He showed me how, and as you can see, I had the start of a nice pile of shucked ears when this picture was taken. No wonder I'm smiling.

It was decided that Jim's city girl wasn't too pathetic when it came to farming, and we did get married.

DOROTHEA WOLFE AKRON, OH

▲ WEDDING GIFT
Newlyweds Wilbert and Lula Mae Gibson of Hammond, Louisiana, got a TV from their family in 1954. Nephew Oscar Williams Jr. of Kirkland, Washington, shared the photo. It was the couple's first furniture.

MEMORIES IN BLACK VELVET

My favorite dress has been hanging in the closet for over 50 years. It's a size 6, so there's no hope of ever wearing it again. I keep it for sentimental reasons.

The black velvet, two-piece dress was part of my trousseau. I wore it the evening after our wedding in 1944 when my husband and I went to an upscale restaurant for dinner.

I also wore the dress on our honeymoon, when we traveled by rail from Arizona to Minnesota to visit my Air Force husband's parents while he was on furlough. Like all trains during the war, ours was crowded with servicemen. We had to sleep sitting up.

We stayed overnight in one of Minneapolis' finest hotels and danced to the great Big Band sounds of that era. Of course, I wore my black velvet dress.

Looking at the dress brings back so many happy memories. I will keep it forever.

JEANNE GLASGOW TUCSON, AZ

BUNKING IN A BUNKER

When Jack returned from the war and we married in 1950, we lived in the basement of a house owned by some very nice people. It was one room, connected to a dug-out root cellar with a dirt floor.

The windows were so small, Jack said the cellar reminded him of the enemy bunkers he'd seen overseas.

When our landlords needed something from the root cellar, they'd knock three times, then come down to the basement, parade through our "home" and get what they needed. As nice as the people were, these root cellar trips seemed to come at the most inconvenient times.

The bathroom had no door, only a curtain. Because we were newlyweds and still pretty shy, one of us would step outside when the other was using the facilities.

MARY JO CARLSON RENTON, WA

WITH INTEREST After his wedding in 1945 (above left), Paul Brandt graduated from college in 1948, as seen in the photo with parents and grandparents (above right). He was so surprised when his parents returned his rent money, allowing him and his family to afford a new home (bottom).

PARENTS BANKED ON HIS PERSEVERANCE

At the end of World War II, I was stationed at Fort Benning, Georgia, and my fianceé, Olga, and I decided to marry. My parents were less than thrilled.

I was 22 and needed two years to complete my bachelor's degree. They were afraid I would not finish my schooling after I was discharged.

I assured them we were determined that I finish school and were certain that, between the GI Bill and Olga's working, we could handle the finances.

After graduation in 1948, we returned to my hometown of Indianapolis and I found a job. Dad redecorated a rental property he owned and rented it to us for $60 a month—reasonable but not inexpensive.

During those early years, which included the births of two children, we managed our money very carefully. It wasn't a problem, since we both were Depression kids who grew up watching all of our pennies.

After three years, my job was going well and the rental property was getting cramped for our family. As we tried to figure out a budget for a new house, Mom and Dad shocked us. Dad handed us the passbook for a savings account that, without telling me, he had opened in my name when we started renting from him. In it was every rent payment—I'd never missed one—plus interest.

This certainly helped us reduce the mortgage we had planned for. It was Dad's way of training us to put money away for a rainy day.

Later, I learned that he and Mom had had to live on their savings for two years early on in the Depression.

Handing over that bankbook was their way of saying, "You were right to marry when you did and you have certainly managed your finances well."

PAUL BRANDT AUBURN, AL

Cupid Must Be Kidding

If one thing's for sure, the chubby cherub sure has a good sense of humor! After all, he put these young lovers into some pretty silly situations.

▲ FUN RIDE FOR THE BRIDE

"As newlyweds in 1949, my husband and I left the church after our wedding and found an odd sight waiting for us—a dune buggy!" says Esther Dirks Herman of Franklin, Nebraska. "We cruised around the town of Dolton, South Dakota, before going to our new home. Friends and family set up a table and supper in our machine shed. We ate, visited, and then spent the night at my sister's house before leaving for our honeymoon in the Black Hills the next morning."

➤ WELL-MATCHED

"My future husband, Charlie, and I started going steady in 1954," says Dottie Grose of Millsboro, Delaware. "We wanted to let everyone know we were an item, so we wore a lot of matching sweaters— the 'in' thing back then. These were our favorites. They were black, with pink, white and black argyle. By the way, we were married in 1958—and we still wear matching sweaters."

◀ ONE-ALARM WEDDING

"Not everyone starts married life like this!" writes Doris Steele of Absecon, New Jersey. "My husband, Gus, and I are pictured Aug. 8, 1953, riding to the edge of Pleasantville, New Jersey, on a fire truck. Gus was a member of the West Atlantic City Volunteer Fire Company. Jay Kisselbock, a relative, took this photo—and another one that ran in the newspaper with a caption saying Gus was bored with the idea of a rented limo. Our lives have been blessed ever since!"

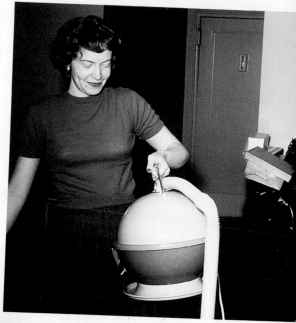

▲ PERFECT GIFT

"For Christmas 1957, my husband gave me a Hoover canister vacuum cleaner," recalls Kathryn Elowitz from Globe, Arizona. "I was very happy to get that vacuum cleaner and used it for 20 years. These days, most women would resent receiving a vacuum for Christmas."

◀ BOOGIE WOOGIE BUGLE GIRL?

"In 1950, my wife, Eunice, and I traveled to Itasca State Park in Minnesota to visit my family," says Curt Nelson of Deerwood, Minnesota. "Eunice and my brother, Paul, enjoyed a 'friendly feud' and were always trying to 'get even.' One morning Eunice really got Paul's goat. She opened Paul's bedroom door while he slept and loudly blew a bugle! Paul chased her out of the house. Still holding the bugle, Eunice stopped to pet our cow. This photo hangs on our wall as a reminder of the early years of our marriage."

Touched by an Angel

UNFORGETTABLE ENCOUNTER

When planning my wedding in my hometown of Granger, Texas, the possibility of my family hosting even a small church wedding did not look promising.

My mother passed away the year before, in 1951, and my father had neither the means for nor the interest to organize such an event. Several of my 10 siblings encouraged me and said they would do what they could. Still, I wondered and worried whether their help would be enough.

Word of my engagement spread quickly in our tiny town of about 1,000, and very soon our church organist approached me. She told me she loved weddings and wanted to do a few things to make ours a memorable one.

Almost immediately, this most elegant and talented lady, Mrs. Mary Scott, quietly took charge. She was ever so sensitive about my feelings, assuring me that her help amounted only to indulging her own penchant for beautiful social occasions.

Mrs. Scott gave a lot of much-needed advice about what was generally proper for the wedding and offered suggestions on handling many of the details.

Even more generously, she provided some things we could never have afforded ourselves, such as a wonderful rehearsal dinner in her home and a profusion of flowers that she arranged herself along the length of the altar rail. Of course, she also played the wedding music to heavenly perfection as I took W.M. Mirtsching to be my husband.

Before the ceremony, when the photographer called for my mother to pose with me for a shot of her adjusting my veil, Mrs. Scott stepped forward without hesitation. She performed the quaint little ritual with motherly grace and charm. (That's us in the photo at left.) What a comforting moment that was for me.

Mrs. Scott's son and daughter-in-law, John William Jr. and Nancy, still live in Granger. I hope they find joy in remembering why people loved and admired Mrs. Scott as an incredibly kind and generous person.

HELEN RISTER MIRTSCHING DALLAS, TX

JUNE BRIDE Jim Palella of Toms River, New Jersey, photographed Mary and Vance Fiorella's wedding party June 26, 1959, at St. Mary Mother of Jesus Roman Catholic Church on Coney Island, Brooklyn, New York. Jim's wife, Frances, a lifelong friend of Mary's, is the bridesmaid in blue. Vance had met Mary while playing in the wedding band for Frances' brother, Jim Rigano.

MODERN CONVENIENCE "In 1941, as a new bride in my first small apartment, I received this stove," says Irma Bauer Foster of Chesterton, Indiana. "I don't remember what make the stove was, but I know it fit perfectly in our kitchen. Our rent was $25 a month."

CHAPTER 5

Where the Heart Is

No matter how far we travel, there really is no place quite like home. Be it an off-the-beaten-path farmhouse or a big-city apartment, home holds the key to countless memories of time spent with family, friends and neighbors in a spot where we'll always feel welcome.

Home Sweet Home

PLENTY OF ROOM FOR MEMORIES

CHOCOLATE HOSPITALITY

A trip to the candy shop didn't take very long when I was growing up in the '40s—the shop was in our house!

My father's Candy Cottage shared a building with our family home in Clinton, Massachusetts. My dad, Michael Biskaduros, began learning the candy-making trade in Sayville, New York, after emigrating from Greece at age 16.

That's Dad in the photo (bottom, right) with my son Michael, taken in 1961. At 80 pounds, the white chocolate bunny was bigger than Michael! The bunny was for sale but never had any takers, so Dad melted it down and used the chocolate for smaller candies.

Michael remembers the day he had his picture taken with a huge white chocolate egg that same year. "Boy, was I nervous that the egg might slip out of my lap!" he said. A special candy mold was used to make the delicate confection, and it was a long, painstaking process.

"Oscar" was another member of our candy-making family. One day when he was stirring the kettle on the store's front porch, two ladies came up and asked what he was making. Were they ever surprised when they realized he was actually a mannequin!

Dad had found Oscar in a store basement. Always on the lookout for promotional gimmicks, he put Oscar in chef's garb and added a motor so he could stir the kettle.

Growing up in a candy shop sure gave me lots of sweet memories!

ARISTEA BISKADUROS GEORGESON CLINTON, MA

WHAT A TREAT The author's son, Michael, got up close to some of Grandpa's extra-large chocolates in 1961. Meanwhile, Oscar, a motorized mannequin (above), kept shoppers smiling.

A YEAR IN "TRAILER CITY"

My dad was a union pipe fitter, and our family moved frequently because he had to go where there was work. We rarely stayed in one place more than a year. By age 10, I knew more about America's cities and states and their topography than most adults.

In the early 1950s, plans were announced for a munitions plant to be built between Augusta, Georgia, and Aiken, South Carolina. Workers were needed to build it, as there were more construction jobs than qualified people in the area.

To house the new workers and their families, the federal government leased large tracts of land and hauled in hundreds of trailers. Trailer cities were created, each with its own sewage treatment plant, water storage tank, grocery store and laundry. These cities were huge. The one where we lived, in Aiken, and another in Augusta held 1,300 trailers each, with a population of 3,000 to 4,000.

The trailers were 27 feet long and 8 feet wide and came in two colors, blue and green. Each had one bedroom, a shower, toilet and a kitchen with a table that folded into the wall. There was also a couch that opened into a bed.

Trailers were just 5 yards apart. That was a good thing for me when I was lucky enough to get a paper route. Although I had 750 papers to deliver, it only took me about two hours.

It was a good place to live.

PARKING-LOT LIVING

The author (right) lived in Robbins Trailer City, shown in an aerial shot (below) taken by Morgan Fitz of Augusta, Georgia. Both photos are from 1958.

Many in the trailer city knew each other from other jobs, and some became lifelong friends. The pay was good, too, and everyone had money to spend. Eventually a drive-in movie theater was built, and a carnival also came around frequently to help us spend our money.

When the plant was finished, we all moved on to find other work. The trailers were sold and moved elsewhere. During our travels over the next several years, we looked for but never found the one we lived in.

MOODY GRUBBS HOUSTON, TX

A HOUSEBOAT WAS HER HAVEN

I knew as soon as I woke up on a spring day in 1942 that something was different. It was absolutely quiet. I ran out onto the deck of our houseboat. As far as I could see in every direction, the land was covered with water.

Our houseboat, on which I was born and lived for nine years, was at my father's boatyard on the Delaware River south of Trenton, New Jersey. (I'm on the left with my brother, sister and mom above.) The dock at which our houseboat was moored was completely submerged below murky water. It was very strange and scary to a 4-year-old girl.

I heard noises in the kitchen, so I knew Mom and Dad were up. So I ran upstairs to wake my siblings. They weren't as enthralled because they had seen such floods before.

After breakfast, the boys stacked the rowboat with cages and nets and put on leather gloves and jackets. I asked what they were going to do, and they just said, "Wait and see."

I spent the day watching odd things floating down the river: oil drums, a chicken coop, even a car.

The boys came back after lunch with cages filled with rescued animals—squirrels and raccoons included. My brothers would keep the animals in the cages and feed them until dry land started to reappear. They were real heroes in my young eyes.

At the end of this exciting day, Mother read me the story of Noah and the great flood. I slept well, safe and protected, with the promise of the rainbow.

GENEVIEVE WILLIAMS SNELLVILLE, GA

BOARDINGHOUSE WAS LIKE ONE BIG FAMILY

In the summer of 1941, my father got a temporary construction job in Charlotte, North Carolina. We moved into a local boardinghouse, where my brother, Thomas, and I were the only children.

Thomas was 7 and I was 4, and to my eyes, that weathered gray house looked enormous. The first bedroom to the left was where our family of four lived.

There was only one bathroom on the first floor, so when the men got ready for work in the morning, there was a lot of banging on the door and shouts of "Hurry up in there—I haven't got all day!"

My favorite room was the kitchen. I'd perch on a tall stool while Mrs. Brown bustled about making food for a houseful of hungry men. The tantalizing aromas of her flaky biscuits, simmering stews and luscious pies filled that kitchen, but my favorite treat was a plain hard-boiled egg. No matter how busy she was, Mrs. Brown would cook an egg just for me. She never made me feel I was a nuisance.

In the evenings after a hearty meal in the dining room, the boarders retired to the parlor to listen to the radio. That's where I was nicknamed "Little Radio," as I was always seeking attention with my constant chatter.

In the fall, Mother and I walked Thomas to school. Then we'd stroll downtown. (That's us window shopping at top, left.)

On Dec. 7, Daddy and his co-workers were sent home early. They huddled around the radio, listening to the incredible news of the bombing of Pearl Harbor. Mother made me play in our room since I was too young to understand the enormity of the life-changing situation.

Since all available manpower was now needed for the war effort, the construction job was left unfinished. Soon after, with our suitcases in the front hall and a car waiting to take us back home, we were hugging everyone goodbye.

Suddenly Mrs. Brown called to me from the kitchen. "Wait! I have something for you!"

With tears in her eyes, she handed me a brown paper sack. Looking inside, I saw it was filled with hard-boiled eggs. I put my arms around Mrs. Brown's neck and, for the last time, felt her warmth and love. Living with two young children in one room must have been difficult for my parents, but I have only happy memories.

SYLVIA HILL DINGLER ROANOKE, VA

"We moved into a four-room brownstone flat in New York City in 1943. We shared a bathroom, with a toilet and sink, with the other tenants on the floor. We had our own bathtub, though—a big one with clawed feet. It was in the kitchen and doubled as a table. I remember that tub well because I was in it when my future husband showed up early for our first date. 'Just a minute!' I called as my mother ran in and put the metal cover over the tub."

ZAPHRA RESKAKIS NEW YORK, NY

▲ HOUSEBROKEN

When the owners of this house in Smithville Flats, New York, saw what the 1935 flood did, they turned a lemon into lemonade. Calling it The Crazy House, they charged a dime admission and made a few bucks before it was condemned. Mrs. Ray Caldwell of Newark Valley, New York, shared this curious shot.

▲ STOP FOR A POP

The big seller at this pop stand in Springfield, Illinois, the summer of 1939 was Nehi orange, reports Robert Ennis of Bellevue, Washington. Robert snapped this photo of friends (from left) Noah Dixon, and Billy, George and Bitsy Garvey. They did all right, Robert recalls.

◄ TRIKE TWINS

There was room for two on this tricycle in Binghamton, New York, when Louis Allen (now living in Sarasota, Florida) snapped this shot of sons Steven and Paul.

FIT FOR A PRINCESS ➤

"This elaborate playhouse built by our father for my younger sister Dorothy and me in 1938 had hardwood floors, a window seat, electricity, rugs, frilly curtains and handmade furniture," says Mary Jean Gee, from Franklin, Indiana.

▲ HYDRANT HIJINKS

"In 1945, on Longacre Street in Detroit, a neighbor who worked for the city would occasionally open the hydrant," writes Georgia Browne of Sturgis, Michigan. "We took turns standing in front of it. That's me behind the girl in the black bathing suit."

◄ NEWS HOUNDS

The family of John Kautz avidly read the *Chicago Daily News*. John Jr. (wearing cap) of Fairfield Bay, Kansas, says his father worked there for 51 years.

What's Cookin'

A TASTY TRIP TO YESTERDAY

HOMEMADE ICE CREAM WAS A SUMMER "MUST"

When I was a kid in the 1920s and '30s, my mother made a 2-gallon freezer of ice cream every Saturday during the summer on our farm.

She made all kinds of flavors, including vanilla, lemon and strawberry from our strawberry patch, using ice we cut from our brook in winter and stored in our smokehouse.

My husband, Wayne (left), also enjoyed homemade ice cream when he was growing up. In this photo from 1928, he's turning the crank of the ice cream freezer at his parents' farm while his dad, Walter Wheelhouse, reads the Sunday funnies. These days, Wayne and I still love ice cream, especially when it's homemade.

VIRGINIA WHEELHOUSE
RUSHVILLE, IL

EFFICIENT COOK SHARED TIME-SAVING TIPS

I won a cooking-tip contest in a Los Angeles newspaper in 1954. My entry suggested a way to prepare a week's worth of meals in a short time.

Working as a nurse, I did my cooking for the week on my days off. All I had to do was make a salad and heat previously prepared dishes.

On the day the reporter and photographer visited my home to take this picture (right), they'd missed lunch. After the photos were taken, I cooked the burgers, and the two newspapermen ate everything on the table and then some!

The cookbook I'm holding had a chapter called How to Feed Four on $20 a Week and discussed entertaining without a maid. Times sure have changed!

MARGARET DAVID TUJUNGA, CA

AND CAROL POURED "The Herrala sisters (above, from left), Virginia, Shirley, Marion and Carol, enjoyed a backyard picnic in Ely, Minnesota, in the early '50s," writes Darrel Gander of Hutchinson. "Marion, by this time, had become Mrs. Darrel Gander." White bread sandwiches, plenty of mustard and ketchup, and a pitcher of Kool-Aid—looks yummy!

SAVING THE MEAL This slide sent in by Robert and Esther Pratt from St. Johns, Michigan, carries the note "Bob cooking steak in the rain, 1975."

CAUGHT RED-HANDED "In this 1949 photo, my mother was in the kitchen cleaning strawberries when a little boy who was visiting climbed up to help," says Betty Lou Nelson of Veedersburg, Indiana.

▲ **WATERMELON WEATHER** Roy Breneman (far left), his parents, brother and sister cultivated a refreshing legacy in the 1920s on their Dalton, Wisconsin, farm. "We sold our watermelons and cantaloupes to local stores and house to house," he recalls.

CAN-DO CANNERS ➤
Betty Wickard and her neighbor Sara Igo put up a big batch of tomatoes back in 1938. Betty, now of Yellow Springs, Ohio, recalls that Sara's husband, Harold, took this tasteful photograph.

▲ **COFFEE BREAK**
Neighbors at this 1949 coffee klatch formed a mini United Nations. From left to right, Grace Lemoncelli was Italian, Bertha Puletti was Polish, Alice Sebastianelli was Lithuanian and Ada Paoletti was born in Italy.

◄ COOKIE TESTER
"This is my brother, Jimmy Dunham, at age 8 in 1965," writes Mary Bustos from Palmer, Texas. "He and my dad had just made all these cookies and had spread them out on the table to cool." It looks like temptation may be getting the best of Jimmy.

▲ RECIPE FOR FUN
"When faced with this scene on a November morning in 1960, all we could do was laugh and take a picture!" writes Jean Dentler of Ann Arbor, Michigan. "Our son, Scott, loved to play with his earthmoving trucks and had found the perfect media to move about...a mess of flour and sugar."

Town & Country

SKYSCRAPERS TO GREEN ACRES

LIFE IN A VERTICAL NEIGHBORHOOD

Living on the fifth floor of an apartment building in the Inwood Hill section of Manhattan—without a telephone—was not a problem in the '40s.

There were five families on each floor. If my twin sister, Marilyn, and I wanted to play with someone on our floor, we'd just go into the hall and knock on the friend's door. If we wanted to contact someone on a lower floor, we'd use a hammer to bang the radiator in our apartment. The noise went all the way to the first floor. We had signals for each person, so each friend would know who was being called.

Then we'd meet in the hall to decide what we should play on the sidewalk—jacks, jump-rope, marbles or roller skating. Whatever we did, there were soon 10 other kids out there after they'd seen us from their windows. Best of all, no parents were inconvenienced by having to drive us somewhere.

Another high point of apartment living comes to mind when I look through our photo albums. Most people take pictures of important occasions in their yards with trees, flowers and grass for the background scenery. Whenever our family took pictures for birthdays, holidays or christenings, we went to the roof.

On washday, Mom hung her clothes from lines on the roof. Marilyn and I would take our dolls up there when Mom hung the wash because other mothers and their children would be up there, too.

The roof was where Marilyn and I did our homework, practiced our typing and flew kites. It was also where the older folks who could walk up stairs went to get some fresh air, and where everyone went to cool off on summer nights if we didn't go to Orchard Beach.

When it snowed, all the kids went to the roof to jump in the piles of snow. No one shoveled the roof, so the snow remained there for days.

It was such fun living in that building. I can't imagine having grown up anywhere else.
BLANCHE MCNALLY MCINTOSH
NISKAYUNA, NY

THE HIGH LIFE From practicing for church choir in 1949 (top right) and studying stenography in 1951, to playing in the snow in 1953 and posing with Dad in 1943, the roof was a favorite spot for these twins.

RUNWAY MAINTENANCE Cows (above) were moved to the field behind the barn and hangar to keep the runway grass down. At top right are the author and dog Nippy.

THE FLYING FARMER

During World War II, just before I was born, Dad flew his own airplane for the Coast Guard. After the war, farming became his livelihood, and flying his lifelong hobby. Known to some as the "flying farmer," he owned a two-seat Luscombe-Silvaire, a classy-looking silver plane with a blue stripe the length of each side.

We lived in the little town of Norway, Maine, where the weather permitted us to fly only six months of the year. When spring came, we pushed the airplane out of the hangar, where it proudly sat right in our own backyard. Dad washed it all up and waxed it, checked the oil and filled it with gas. After starting the engine with a few quick pulls to the propeller, he drove the plane out to the road, around the side of the barn and onto the field behind it.

The runway was sometimes a hay field, sometimes a cow pasture. After the haying was done, Dad let the cows onto the field to keep the grass down. And if by chance the cows were grazing there when he wanted to fly, he sent me to round them up

and drive them off the runway.

The field was a rectangle with a north-south orientation. If the windsock on the barn pointed east or west, a takeoff or landing would be difficult.

Mom said that when I was a toddler, the three of us took off in a crosswind. As we approached the end of the field, Mom could see we didn't have the altitude to miss the power lines. She was sure we were going to crash. We missed the wires by mere inches, while I sat there in her lap, intrigued and happy and unaware of any potential danger.

I became Dad's right-hand man on the farm—quite a tomboy I was. One day, I flew with him to town, in our dirty work clothes, to buy a machine part. It was definitely quicker, not to mention more fun, than making the trip in our 2-ton truck. Upon our return, Mom scolded us for not changing into clean clothes.

Sometimes I'd beg Dad to do a loop. He'd rev up the engine, then veer straight up and around in a big circle until we were back where we started. It was such fun.

One day he did it differently. I

FAMILY FLYER This Luscombe-Silvaire, the sports car of lightplanes, belonged to the author's parents, Willard "Bill" and Dorothy Berry.

never knew whether it was just for fun or if he was trying to get my goat. He revved up the engine and started the ascent. But when we reached the top of the loop we remained there, flying upside-down, hanging from our seat belts with sand from the floor falling on us like rain.

Mom was waiting for us when we landed. "What's wrong, honey? You look so pale," she said. Dad just chuckled.

Many years have passed since I flew with Dad. It wasn't until years later that I came to realize what a special thing it was to be the daughter of the "flying farmer."
BETTY BOCKORAS OKEECHOBEE, FL

MEALS ON WHEELS HAVE RURAL FLAVOR

"My parents, Floyd and Harriet, farmed near Marathon, Iowa," says Richard Roder of Aurelia. "During the 1949 oat harvest, my mother would load up our Chevy with a card table and a hot dinner and drive out to the field at noon to meet my father. As soon as they were done eating and listening to the news on a portable radio, Mother cleaned up and Dad was back harvesting. The crops couldn't wait."

▲ HIGH-WIRE ACT

"This is my mother-in-law, Lucille, on washday around 1953," writes Nancy Siria of Arlington Heights, Illinois. "The photo was taken in the Hyde Park area of Chicago, where my husband's family lived for four years."

▲ "BIRDS" ON A BARN

"This photo of my sisters, cousins and me (on the right) was taken at a family get-together one summer day in the late '20s at my aunt and uncle's farm near Kalamazoo, Michigan," says Dorothy Bryer Yarnell of Park Forest, Illinois. "We were perched atop the old barn just like a row of birds."

▲ CAPITOL KIDS

"I was born and raised in the shadow of the Capitol in Washington, D.C.," says Elaine Myers of Berkeley Lake, Georgia. "My family's row house was just blocks from the building. When I was a child, in the 1940s, I knew every corner of the Capitol. Other kids and I would play hide-and-seek and pretend we saw ghosts. In this 1945 photo, I'm with a Capitol page whose name I don't remember."

◄ AS FRESH AS IT GETS

"We grew our own fruits and vegetables when we lived in West Boylston, Massachusetts," writes Ellie Haller McEachern of Deltona, Florida. "There was nothing like being able to pick something fresh to eat. In this photo from 1955, I was out in the field picking corn to serve for supper."

Reader Favorites
A TRUNKFUL OF SURPRISES

THERE'S AN ELEPHANT IN MY GARDEN!

In August 1955, our local fire department sponsored a three-ring circus to come to our town of Middle Granville in upstate New York. The circus set up in a field near the airport, down the road from our house. One act even featured a live trained elephant named Judy.

The circus was a one-day event. So that night, the tent was taken down and the equipment removed. The only things left were a tractor-trailer that transported the elephant and her trainer, and a motor home that served as the manager's home and office.

The next morning, I looked out my window and spotted an odd-looking mound in our garden. Curious, I went down for a closer look.

When I got near the garden, I saw a huge ear come up. Then I saw a trunk—the trunk of a full-grown, onion-eating elephant!

Oh, my gosh! I thought. *I've got an elephant in my garden. A real live elephant!*

I drove the short distance to the circus and woke up the sleepy-eyed manager.

"Sir," I said, "are you missing an elephant?"

"Go to the trailer and get the trainer," he told me.

I found the trainer, and we rushed back to my house. He had no problem getting Judy up and out of the garden. In fact, he had her do some tricks for my wife and our sons while I took photos so my friends would believe my story. It's safe to say that Judy was the most unexpected guest we ever had!

EDWARD TATKO MIDDLE GRANVILLE, NY

ELEPHANTINE PROBLEM
In 1955, Ed Tatko (right) found an elephant in his garden (at top). Before the trainer took the animal back to the circus, Ed snapped some photos, which appeared in the local paper.

BASEBALL BREAK This young ballplayer was taking the "Home Sweet Home" message above him literally. "My brother, Howard Hansen, was taking a much-needed rest in the comfort of our North Dakota home after a day of baseball practice in 1962," says Leslie Hansen from Anoka, Minnesota.

BUDGET TRAVELS Back in the '30s, Leila Williams lived in the country with her mother and grandmother. "Most of the time, we didn't have a car, so we hitchhiked to town," she writes from her home in Zanesville, Ohio. "Eventually, Mom and I became tourists in this manner, hitchhiking from Ohio to Washington, D.C., and then to California. For the D.C. trip, we only had $3 for 3 days, staying in a YWCA dormitory for 25 cents each. We went to California with $37, and we slept outdoors on blankets that we carried everywhere with us. Once in the Los Angeles area, we stayed in cabins for 75 cents a night. It sure was a different world back then!"

CHAPTER 6

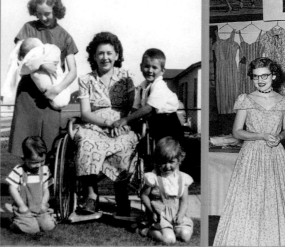

Getting by in
Tough Times

During trying times, such as the Great Depression,
families pulled together—banking on courage,
determination and unshakable love to see them through.
Recycling was a way of life, and as people's mettle
was tested, everyday heroes were born.

What Money Can't Buy

EVEN IN HARD TIMES THEY BROUGHT JOY TO OTHERS

SINGING THROUGH THE DEPRESSION

In the 1920s and '30s, St. Petersburg, Florida, was a winter haven for snowbirds from the United States and Canada. My father moved the family from Vancouver, British Columbia, to participate in the big real estate boom.

Instead, we arrived in St. Petersburg just in time for the big bust—better known as the Great Depression!

Although jobs were scarce, we managed to survive. A major source of income was our family orchestra.

My talented mother, a professional musician, opened a music studio and a musical kindergarten in our new home. Those of us in the family were her first pupils.

A pianist and vocalist, Mother taught us to sing in harmony, read music and play the piano. Later, my older sister, Beth, learned to play the cello; my older brother, Sam, played the violin; Dad played the bass fiddle; and I played a mean second violin. (That's us in the photo at right.)

At first, we were known as The Five Musical Haights, but a younger sister and brother eventually came along and then we were seven. With the exception of Dad and me, everyone in the family had a natural musical talent.

Beth and I also learned to dance. She excelled in tap dancing, and I did well with acrobatics and tumbling. We all were given drama lessons.

At the time, St. Petersburg had a great number of clubs for snowbirds. There was one named for each state in the union—the Vermont Club, the Ohio Club, etc.

All winter, we'd perform at different hotels and clubs, doing two or three programs a week. Dad and Mom wrote our scripts, and the comedy program was in the form of a play about a family's dress rehearsal for a performance.

In addition to the classical music we played, the four-part harmony we sang and our lively dance numbers, the script provided dialogue for the usual horseplay in families.

Even though it was the Depression, life was fun. Every morning we got up early and met in the music room to practice. Playing music together made us a tight-knit family, and we remained close all our lives.

Even though we were as poor as many other families, we children never knew it. At Christmas, we'd visit the orphanage and an old people's home to give free programs.

Along with our musical instruments and costumes, Dad loaded boxes of oranges and other fruit to take along as gifts. We'd even wrap up last year's toys that Dad had repaired and repainted to give to the children. We thought we were rich!

Now, I know that we truly were.

EILEEN HAIGHT MULVIHILL
LOWER LAKE, CA

KINDHEARTED FAMILY Since her family had no camera of its own in the 1930s, the author has just one photo (at left) of her and her mother, Christine Schnetzle, together, from 1932. The author's brother, Bob, is pictured with their mother (above) and with the author (below).

THE NAPKIN LADY

At night, you could see their firelight flickering in the distance along the railroad tracks that ran through the middle of our small town of Harrison, just outside of New York City.

The men hovering around these campfires became known as hoboes. The sad-faced, disheveled-looking men were part of the millions who lost their jobs during the decade or so of the Great Depression.

Nearly one out of every four workers in the United States could not find a job, and there was no unemployment insurance back then to help them out. Thousands became homeless, losing hope and becoming desperate.

Many people left families behind with relatives and struck out for places unknown. They'd wrap whatever belongings they could carry in a bandanna that dangled from the end of a long stick that rested on the shoulder as they walked the rails or jumped freight trains from town to town.

They hoped to find work or, if not that, they at least hoped to find a kind person who would offer them food or drink to sustain them until the next day, when they would look for work again.

Every once in a while, one or two of these people would come into our town searching for work. Just a few were lucky and found short-term jobs, but most did not.

On their walk through town, they would stop at homes to ask for food. The lady of the house usually tried to do what she could for them, but many of the men in these households were also unemployed, and food was scarce.

Although money was tight in our home, whenever one of these men came to our door, my mother would fix the man a sandwich and a glass of milk. There was a card table on our back porch, and Mom would set them up there. She felt so sorry for these men that she would put the sandwich on a nice dish, along with a white paper napkin, "to give them a little respect," she would say.

Whenever the men wanted to talk, Mom would sit with them and hear all about their families. Sometimes, they would pull well-worn pictures out of their pockets.

One day, a year or two after the Depression subsided, we received a letter addressed simply to "The Napkin Lady." Of course, no one knew what that meant. Mom opened the mysterious letter, and to her amazement, it was from one of the men she had fed.

He wanted to thank her again for her kindness when he so

desperately needed it. He said that the napkin she placed beside his dish had made him think of home and how much he missed his family and his loved ones. He explained that it suddenly dawned on him that when he was home, he had everything but money, but on the road, he had nothing.

So he decided to return home to his family and try again to make a go of it, this time with his family at his side. He wrote that he had a job and was beginning to see the light of day.

Tears ran down my mother's face as she finished reading the letter. It made her feel humble and happy at the same time—to think that such a small gesture would have such an impact on someone's life, someone she couldn't even remember.

But that's how my mom was, always giving, always caring. She was such a wonderful influence upon us children, and apparently, upon strangers as well.

JOAN STUER WETHERSFIELD, CT

DAD WORKED A COAL MINE… IN OUR HOUSE!

I was a curious young child who wanted to explore the "cave" Daddy had made off our mudroom, but suspicion ruled that females in a coal mine were bad luck—yep, a coal mine.

Perhaps I should begin my story again. The 1930s and early '40s on our farm in Bridgeport, Ohio, were as wonderful as I could have hoped for.

My dad, Clarence Baxter, worked for Wheeling Steel in Beach Bottom, West Virginia, and also worked hard on our farm to raise his five children: George, Edward, Alberta, Vivian and me.

One day while Dad was digging out a basement and making our furnace room larger, he hit a vein of coal. Bringing carbide lights and wheelbarrows, he and my brothers kept digging with picks and shovels until that vein became our personal coal mine—right off the mudroom next to our kitchen.

Dad braced the mine with locust logs, which lasted much longer than other wood, and made a special drain for excess water. He also dug a vault in the mine to hide extra money.

Dad used dynamite to loosen the coal. My youngest sister, now Vivian Stevens, remembers our neighbor running to our house, yelling, "He's shaking the dishes off my shelves!"

We had a few cave-ins and would have to haul the dirt out in wheelbarrows, then shore up the ceiling with new locust logs.

Vivian recalls a time when Dad came out of the mine and said to her, "Bib, run and get some white clothes and water, and whatever you do, don't call your mother."

Not paying any attention, Vivian looked up, saw Dad's face covered with blood and started screaming, "Mom, Mom, Mom!"

A piece of coal had hit Dad in the head, causing a gash—the worst accident he ever had in the mine. Of course, our mother came and cleaned the wound the best she could.

A story about our mine was published with pictures in the *Hanna Coal News,* a small-town coal newspaper, in December 1938. The overzealous reporter had Alberta hold a coffeepot next to the mudroom stove and pretend the mudroom was our kitchen. This was very embarrassing to my mother, as her kitchen sparkled with cleanliness and held the coal-fired double-oven stove.

In 1950, after Dad passed away, we had another cave-in and our mother wouldn't open up the mine again. That was the end of our mine, but it had served very well for many years.

As Vivian likes to say, we were the original "coal miner's daughters"!

MARY BAXTER STOETZER NORTH FORT MYERS, FL

THE DAY ELEANOR ROOSEVELT STOPPED TO VISIT

I'll never forget the special visitor who arrived at our house without warning one day.

Born in 1921, I grew up a child of the Great Depression and was the youngest of 13. Our family was uprooted in 1927 and forced to relocate in the little coal-mining town of Cassville, West Virginia, where my father and older brothers were lucky to find jobs. (That's me in the photo at right at age 15.)

Franklin D. Roosevelt became president in 1933, but it took a while for some of his many social improvement projects to get rolling. One of them was related to our community center.

There, shoes, fabrics and merchandise from bankrupt factory warehouses found a place in our sewing centers, which were set up to make clothing and distribute it to the needy. Women from the town, including Mamma, sewed long hours, making everything from flannel undergarments to housedresses.

We were happy that President Roosevelt also initiated the distribution of dried milk and sacks of flour to the needy.

You see, my mother used to make bread once or twice a week, and now she had dried milk to put in our bread. It was wonderful, and I helped bake bread often for family meals.

In fact, I was baking bread on a hot July day when a stranger appeared at our old patched screen door and knocked. Being 11 years old, I was somewhat startled by this, as most neighbors just walked in and hollered out your name whenever they needed you.

I was removing hot bread from the oven and turning it out onto clean bleached flour sacks when I saw her standing at our door. She was a tall woman with gray-brown hair, thick and curly.

She smiled, and she asked if my mother was at home.

When Mamma came to the door, the stranger introduced herself as Eleanor and called my mother by name!

"My husband, Franklin, has asked me to stop by and see how you folks are doing and if there's anything else he can do to be of assistance," she said kindly.

Mamma opened the door and the two women shook hands. Mamma led the first lady to our old round oak table, covered with an oiled tablecloth, and they each took a seat.

On the table was a bowl of our homemade black cherry jam, some poorly mixed oleomargarine and a single can of evaporated milk.

As they sat down, Mamma asked Mrs. Roosevelt if she would like a cup of coffee. With a big smile, Eleanor Roosevelt answered, "Yes, please."

Then she sniffed the fresh bread and said, "My, but that bread really smells delicious."

I cut a few slices of that hot bread, then put them on a small plate that we'd received inside a box of oatmeal. I was amused to see our first lady slather oleo and jam, then wipe her mouth on a piece of bleached flour sack.

Next Mrs. Roosevelt asked what happened to the scraps of material left after the garments were made at the community center. Mamma said they weren't wasted—the ladies took them home and worked them into quilt tops. The first lady asked if, by chance, we had one and if she could see it.

As Mamma retrieved a quilt, Mrs. Roosevelt asked me about

Louisa Yocum -15 yrs. 1936

my schooling and the lunch program, and encouraged me to remain in school, no matter how difficult it was.

"Education is a warehouse of knowledge that never empties," I remember her saying.

When Mamma returned with the quilt, the two women unfolded it and examined it closely. Mrs. Roosevelt smiled again and asked Mamma if she would consider selling it.

"No, I cannot sell it to you, but I will be happy to give it to you," Mamma said. "Tell the president we wish to thank him for all the ways he has helped us, and we are grateful."

Mrs. Roosevelt patted the quilt draped over her arm as she walked out the door.

"Thank you," she said. "Franklin will be pleased to hear this report. I've had a very pleasant afternoon."

THELMA LOUISE PIERPOINT
STREETSBORO, OH

Making Do

DESPERATE TIMES LED TO HEARTFELT MEMORIES

BELOVED SATIN
The dress worn
by the author
in this colorized
class photo was
made possible
by her aunt
Clovis Kornegay
(above left).

HAND-ME-DOWN WITH
A SILVER LINING

Today I heard Dolly Parton's beautiful song
"Coat of Many Colors," and once again it
brought back a cherished memory of my
very own childhood.

My mother was the single parent of three
girls and a boy. We lived in Little Rock,
Arkansas, where Mama worked as a waitress.
I was the youngest, just 3 years old, when
she got a divorce from our abusive father.

Mama found it so hard to keep a roof over
our heads that in 1945 she moved us out
to the country, where she had two brothers
to help her make ends meet. We lived near
Jonesboro in shotgun houses on the Tulot
and Judd Hill plantations. In the winter,
howling winds and snow crept through the
cracks of our houses; in the summer, Mama
had to shoo flies away from the food.

Mama and my teenage siblings, Alice
and Jim, did all they could to plant, hoe,
pick and pull cotton bolls from the hard,
unyielding ground. Of course, the only
clothes we had were hand-me-downs, or
maybe a pretty handmade flour sack dress.

When I was 8 years old, my wonderful
aunt from Little Rock came to visit. She
was very small and gave me an old coat of
hers with a lovely wine-colored satin lining.
Mama took the lining from the coat and, by
hand, sewed me a beautiful little dress with
two rows of lace down the front.

I was so proud of that dress—and when
the teacher of our two-room schoolhouse
said it was the prettiest dress she had ever
seen, I was even more thrilled.

When we had school pictures taken
that year, Mama combed my hair and
dressed me in my satin dress. To this day, I
don't know where the money came from
to buy the pictures. But I still smile and
occasionally shed a tear when I look at that
picture and remember how I loved that
dress made from a coat lining.
NITA LYNN-ZAHN SHREVEPORT, LA

IT'S NOT BURNT…
IT'S "HEINS BROWN"!

The Heins family never went hungry during the Depression. Dad was a teacher and luckily never lost his job. Still, we often heard the admonitions "Food is money—don't waste it!" and "Waste not, want not!"

That explains how my brothers and I came to like cookies and toast dark. Most people would call it burnt, but we called it "Heins brown."

In the late '20s and early '30s, Mother baked bread, and we never ate it without toasting it.

Dad would sit at the head of the table with a "flip-flop" toaster at his elbow. He'd put the bread onto the door of the toaster, tilt it closed and watch until a wisp of smoke emerged. Then he'd let the door down, flip the bread over and tip the door back toward the heating element to toast the other side of the bread.

Toast made that way was just as good as any toaster could make it today—if you paid attention!

The problem was, everyone in our family was a talker, so conversations at mealtimes were always intense and interesting—so interesting that Dad often forgot he was supposed to be watching the toaster.

The first family member to spot the smoke would yell "TOAST!" Dad would then rescue the almost-blackened slice.

The person for whom the toast was intended faced a choice—either eat it that way or take it to the kitchen, scrape off the black into the sink, then come back to the table and eat the toast with scrape marks where the black had been.

Of course, throwing away the toast was never an option. We almost always chose to eat the piece as it came from the toaster. Over the years, that choice became habit, and habit became preference. To this day, we all like our toast Heins brown (almost black).

Toast wasn't the only food we learned to love semi-burnt. Every Saturday, Mother baked a big batch of cookies. Each of us kids was allowed one cookie after dinner each day.

At our house, you did not sneak cookies between meals.

But there was one circumstance that would help us satisfy our cookie cravings.

If Mother accidentally left a sheet of cookies in the oven until they were deep brown or black, she couldn't bring herself to put the "spoiled" cookies in the cookie jar, where they'd shame her for the rest of the week. So we got to eat the evidence!

It didn't take very long for my older brother, Sterling, and me to devise a scheme that would get us a glorious bunch of Heins brown cookies fresh from the oven.

The two of us could almost always think of some activity that would draw Mother's attention from her baking at a critical time and cause her to burn a sheet or two of cookies.

I'll never know whether or not she had our little scheme figured out and just went along with the game to grant us the thrill of undeserved treats. Regardless, the result was a lifelong love for cookies that are almost black on the bottom and toast that has that delicious Heins brown.

HOLLYS HEINS HEER AMES, IA

CAREFUL WHAT YOU WISH FOR

It was a scorching hot afternoon in Smyrna, Georgia. Even the birds and bees were still.

Old Maid was no fun. "Captain, May I" had lost its challenge, and it was too hot to play kick the can. Even the lemonade was a little sour. In short, we were bored.

This was not the usual situation for my sister, brother and me. Although it was 1934 and we had little money for entertainment, the Depression was never that hard on us.

But this particular afternoon we were feeling sorry for ourselves. We imagined other children at summer camp, enjoying all the many activities we did not have at home.

Being the oldest, I decided to approach our mother about our particular situation.

"We want to go to summer camp," I complained. "We want to have fun like the other children."

I should have known better than to present a challenge like that to my mother. Without batting an eye, she replied, "You want to go to summer camp? We'll have summer camp right here at home."

That next morning, the three of us kids were greeted with the following schedule posted on the kitchen door:

Reveille	7:00
Breakfast	7:15
Room Inspection	8:00
First Activity Period	9:00
Second Activity Period	10:00
Swimming	11:00
Lunch	12:00
Rest Hour	1:00
Crafts	2:30
Free Time	4:30
Supper	6:00
Front Porch Games	7:00
Taps	8:30

Leave it to our mother. Her fertile mind designed a plan a camp director would have been proud of, including a few special improvisations of her own.

The first activity period turned out to be preparing vegetables for lunch and for canning. We shucked corn, shelled butter beans and black-eyed peas, peeled peaches and even quartered apples.

To create a little competition, we divided the vegetables into three piles and raced to see who would finish first.

For the second activity, we baked—corn bread, rolls, pies, cakes, cookies and bread. One benefit, though, was that we got to eat what we baked.

Swimming was in a small canvas pool with about a foot of water in it. It was better than nothing, but not much.

After a lunch of meat and the very vegetables we prepared ourselves, we were sent to bed for an hour and a half of rest.

The two-hour craft period was taken up learning sewing skills—knitting, embroidery, quilting and needlepoint. We still have quilts from that summer's "crafts."

After supper, we gathered on the porch for a game of counting cars. One team counted the cars going in one direction, and the other team took the opposite direction. The team that reached 20 cars first won.

Our house faced Highway 41, which at the time was the only road between Atlanta and Marietta. Still, in those days, it sometimes took as long as half an hour for 20 cars to pass.

Soon it was bedtime, and camp began all over again the next morning. We adhered to the schedule all summer, although we complained bitterly of it much of the time.

Before it was over, I wished I'd never heard of summer camp—and my sister and brother stayed mad at me the whole time!

Today I look back with amazement. During that one summer, I learned all the skills I later needed to run a house.

I still marvel at the cunning of our mother, who was clever enough to use our time of discontent to such creative ends.
ELEANOR DABNEY AUSTELL, GA

FEED BAG *Fashions*

"THE COTTON KID"

I had become good friends with four other girls through the Bracken County High School 4-H Club, based in Brooksville, Kentucky.

During the summer of 1952, we entered a contest sponsored by Louisville's *Courier-Journal* newspaper at the Kentucky State Fair. It was a sewing contest for fashions made entirely from feed sacks.

Because I was making a formal, I needed more feed sacks than the other girls. I wasn't very busty, so I took out seams and darts so many times that the fabric would wear out. It was a good thing that the feed bags were very strong.

One day, the county agent stopped by to see how we were progressing. When he was told of my problem, he laughed and said, "What nature's forgotten, stuff with cotton." That became our catchphrase for the summer, and I was dubbed "the cotton kid."

Several days after entering our outfits in the contest, we received a call that we had won and we all made the drive for this newspaper picture. That's me, Laura Lou Lenox, on the left. Also standing, from left, are Phylis Charles in a church dress, Norma Weiss in a school dress and Helen Fleeman in her play outfit. Seated is Roberta Dennis in her sleeping outfit.

Our prize was a sewing machine, which we used for class projects the next two years.

We have all married and most of us have moved away, but the picture still brings back great memories of that summer.

LAURA MONSON COLD SPRING, KY

CHICKEN CONDOS "During the Depression, to help support our family, my father built this large henhouse and raised chickens, delivering eggs to people in our town of Merrimac, Massachusetts," writes Claire Duffy of Green Harbor. "That's me at the age of 3 with my 6-year-old brother, Val, in 1933. When the economy picked up and Dad got a job in a local shoe factory, he tore down the henhouse and used the lumber to build a cottage at Hampton Beach, New Hampshire. We'd rent the cottage out to folks in the summer and enjoy it when it wasn't occupied."

▲ EVERYBODY IN THE POOL!

"My dad, Ernest Sidenstricker (wearing the boater), could build anything with salvaged pieces and parts," says Jack Sidenstricker of Leipsic, Ohio. "In 1935, he built my two sisters and me a teeter-totter, a covered sandbox and this swimming pool at our home in Carey, Ohio. On a hot summer day, most of the neighborhood kids joined the fun. I'm fifth from right. My sister Denelda is to my left, and sister Patty is third from my right."

◄ A BIT OF HORSING AROUND

"My father-in-law, Jay Darling of Grand Rapids, Michigan, once worked for people who paid him with a Shetland pony," writes Claudette Darling of Comstock Park, Michigan. "Jay took out the backseat of his 1937 Ford and the pony was put in. I imagine there were a lot of heads turning, jaws dropping and fingers pointing as passers-by witnessed the 'passenger.'"

▲ ONE STYLE FITS ALL?

That seems to be the case for this photo, taken in 1929 or '30 in Canute, Oklahoma. Pauline Hutson Mackie of Everett, Pennsylvania (front row, far right), says, "Mama would break an egg on the head of each of us girls to wash our hair." The boy in front is Pauline's cousin Oscar Lee Neice, and the girl in back at far left was an unknown friend. The other daughters of Frank and Mabel Hutson were (from left) Maxine Weems, Easter Matthews and Lucille Turner.

◄ AGITATING ACTION

Frank Hecht built this small tractor from parts he found around the family farm when he was 11 years old. "That's my dad, Albert, with me in the photo," he writes from Tilden, Nebraska. "However, money was scarce in 1936, and we certainly couldn't afford a motor for my tractor. One day, when my folks were gone, I took the motor out of my mom's Maytag washing machine and belted it to the tractor's rear wheel. When my mother came home, she asked me where I found the motor. It didn't take me long to get the motor back in the washing machine."

Heroes with Heart

COMPASSION PREVAILED IN TOUGH TIMES

HANDY, NOT HANDICAPPED

Our mother had six children and was confined to a wheelchair, but there was never a job that she couldn't tackle.

Given that she was only 18 years old and already the mother of a toddler when she was stricken with polio, I marvel that she did not become bitter and helpless. Some might have done that, but not Frances Mercedes McCowan (later Mrs. Jack McCoy). She not only emerged

from an iron lung—to which doctors thought she would be confined all her life—but challenged her nurses and therapists to push her harder.

During her months at a rehabilitation facility for polio patients of the 1930s and '40s in Warm Springs, Georgia, Mom built the kind of character that helped her meet challenges and live life to the fullest.

As a homemaker in Torrance, California, during the 1950s, Mom

was always designing things to help her accomplish everyday endeavors such as cooking, cleaning and laundry. If there was a way to overcome an obstacle, Mom would find it or invent it herself!

She had my dad build her a foldout ironing board she could wheel herself up to when it was set at the right height. In later years, she had a stovetop designed the same way.

Her creativity did not end with household tasks but extended into disciplining her children. We knew we couldn't outrun her. If we got into trouble, Mom would get the broom, aim it carefully at the tush and—*whop!*—we had a reminder that she was in charge.

Most of the time, though, her loving entreaties to do something were enough for us.

We had a lot of good times sightseeing and camping. Mom loved roughing it, and she cooked great meals outdoors. The smile on her face told us that she adored watching us play, enjoying the things she herself could not do.

Her lessons gave way to a legacy I passed to my children: to work hard, share with others and be grateful for what you have.

Mother passed away just before her 50th birthday. I know she would be proud that her six children taught their own children what it means to overcome adversities. What greater love can a mother give her children than to set such a fine example?

ROBERTA MERSHON
RIO RANCHO, NM

THE BURNETTE FAMILY Pictured are Minnie Burnette (below) in 1970 and her six children (clockwise from top left), Elmer, William, Andrew, Myrtle, Luther and Blanche, sometime in the 1950s.

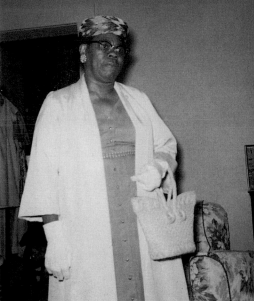

MAMMA MINNIE VALUED EDUCATION ABOVE ALL

During the '30s, the economy of the rural South was based on family farming. Children often missed school while they helped bring in the crops.

My mother-in-law, Minnie Burnette, and her husband, Ellis, farmed on land they owned in Arkansas. Minnie believed in the value of education. Her eldest of six children, Elmer, recalled an example.

Elmer was getting ready for school one day when his father said, "Minnie, the boy can't go to school today. I need help with the plowing and I've got to get the planting started."

Mamma Minnie, always calm and reasoned, said nothing. She quietly prepared Elmer's lunch and saw that he left the house on time. Then she said to Ellis, "He needs to go to school, Ellis. But don't worry, I'll do his work."

At the time, no one knew that Minnie was pregnant. But she plowed the fields that day and on many others.

In 1930, Ellis died. Relatives suggested that Minnie break up the family to ease her "burden." She refused.

It was a difficult time. But everyone worked hard to survive. Even the youngest, Luther, then 5 (he's now my husband), had chores each day.

The children also continued to go to school. After graduation from eighth grade, they had to attend the junior high school in Brinkley, 5 miles away.

There was no transportation for "colored" children, so two of them, Blanche and Bill, boarded in town.

"We returned home every weekend," Blanche recalls. "My mother paid for our rooms and sent food from the farm. I did the cooking for Billy and me until we completed our studies."

In 1936, the heavily mortgaged farm was lost and the family was forced to move into Brinkley.

There they lived in a rent-to-own house. Mamma Minnie valued home ownership as much as education, and worked two jobs to pay the $10-a-month mortgage until the house became her very own.

Mamma Minnie worked as a counter girl in a restaurant and as a maid in a hotel. But at harvesttime, she took the children to the fields with her to earn even more money.

Minnie died in 1981. Elmer became the teacher she always wanted in the family. In fact, 12 family members became educators, including Elmer's eldest grandson, who recently retired as a college president.

Mamma Minnie's precious legacies of education and home ownership continue to be highly valued in the family. Most of her descendants hold undergraduate degrees and are homeowners.

Minnie Burnette is gone, but she will never be forgotten.
GEORGIA BURNETTE AMHERST, NY

DOC'S DAIRY ALWAYS DELIVERED THE GOODS

It was bitter cold that January evening in 1932. We lived in a modest uninsulated frame house on First Street in Wenatchee, Washington.

It took three stoves to heat our home. The dining room was warmed by a small oil stove, and a potbellied stove stood in the parlor. In the kitchen was the South Bend Malleable, which Mother used to cook our meals and heat water.

To me, those stoves used an extraordinary amount of wood, because at age 9, I had the job of filling our wood boxes. That kept me moving back and forth along the 60-foot path to the woodshed.

This particular evening, I banked the kitchen and parlor stoves so they'd continue to burn. This meant loading them full and adjusting the damper to keep a slow fire burning.

We went to bed early that night, and I could tell something was troubling Mother, although I didn't know what it was. Since my bedroom was right over the parlor, it usually stayed warm up there, but this night was different.

Around 4 a.m., I heard my parents' alarm clock go off. As I moved slightly in bed, I discovered that the sheets only a fraction of an inch from where I lay were like ice. Gingerly, I moved back to the spot I'd warmed and made a mental note not to move again. It was cold—*really cold!*

I heard the door to the parlor stove open and a poker stirring the embers. My parents were discussing something, but so softly I couldn't hear what they were saying.

Then, off in the distance, I heard a truck with a broken tire chain clanking against the underside of a fender. I knew it had to be the milk truck of Dr. Lester from Lester's Dairy.

We called him "Doctor" because he was a veterinarian as well as being owner and deliveryman of the dairy. He had several other customers up the street, so he'd drive and stop, drive and stop—the broken chain clanking louder and louder as his truck approached.

Finally he arrived in front of our house. Dr. Lester's boots crunched across our snow-packed yard, then onto the porch. I could hear the sound of the glass bottles being set into the device we'd hung on the side of the house to keep the cat from getting into the milk.

Then I heard something I didn't expect. The door opened and Mother asked Dr. Lester to step inside. She was talking in a voice so low I couldn't understand what she was saying.

But I could hear Dr. Lester's reply. "I know you're behind on your bill," he said. "But everybody is, and I have to milk those cows anyway. You have children who need this milk. If you're worrying about the bill, don't!

"Let *me* worry about the bill," he added. "This economic situation can't last much longer. Pay me when you're able."

With that, the door opened and shut again, and I heard the chain clank off down the street. Two days later, a quarter-pound of butter appeared with our milk. We hadn't ordered it, and I doubt we were ever charged for it.

Years later, we learned it wasn't just our family that Dr. Lester treated with such kindness. Many others were helped through those difficult times thanks to the generosity and concern of a wonderful man who, morning after morning, delivered the milk of human kindness.

DELBERT GRAHAM
PORT TOWNSEND, WA

WHEELS OF HARD FORTUNE

Weather permitting, I always rode my bike around the neighborhood after school. Bikes were not common in our neighborhood of Shawnee, Oklahoma, in 1937, and to have one was to be set apart. You were someone to be admired and envied by other children, and I relished their looks when they saw me riding by.

I had just ridden my precious Christmas bicycle down the alley into our backyard and carefully leaned it against the back of the house.

As I entered the house that March day, my mother met me and said my father was home after several days of work in the oil fields, and he needed to talk to me. She told me to go up to my bedroom and wait for him.

I was a very worried young boy as I went upstairs, and when I heard my father slowly climbing the stairs, I was filled with apprehension. In our family, father-son talks usually meant I had done something wrong.

My father came in and sat down on the bed beside me. He said my mother was going to have a baby, and because of medical bills and other expenses, they could not afford to make the payments on my bicycle. We needed to return it to the Oklahoma Tire and Supply store where they had bought it.

I was crushed. What could I tell my friends? What would they think when they found out that I no longer had a bicycle?

I went downstairs to get the bike, wheeled it around to the car and then helped my father put it into the backseat. My mom, with a mother's great wisdom, opened the passenger door and suggested that I ride downtown with my father.

When we pulled up in front of the store, we got the bicycle out and I wheeled it across a seemingly endless expanse of yellow linoleum. I gave it to a grim-faced man who was waiting for us, and while he and Dad talked, I went back out and got into the car, immersed in self-pity.

As my father wordlessly pulled away from the store, I looked over and saw his strained, taut face. For some reason, I slid across the seat and leaned up against him. He put his arm around me and held me close all the way home, moving his arm only to shift gears.

He was my father. I loved him, and I knew he loved me, too. Suddenly, all was bright and warm in my world.

My father was a very strong, hardworking, courageous man, a much-respected oil-field driller with years of experience working 12-hour days, seven days a week. He had served with distinction as first sergeant of a machine-gun company in France during World War I, whose horrors he seldom spoke about.

Yet today, as a father and grandfather myself, I often think that one of the bravest things my father ever did was to slowly climb those old wooden stairs in Depression-stricken Oklahoma to tell a young son that his bicycle had to go back.

My father was killed in an automobile accident in 1953, but I know today he still loves me, and I know I still love him. Whenever I think of that, suddenly all is bright and warm in my world once again.

DONALD KEITH DUBBS MINEOLA, TX

Reader Favorites
FRUGAL STRATEGIES LED TO SUCCESS

THE COUPON QUEEN

In the mid-1940s, Ann Cox Williams was the original extreme couponer. Through savvy shopping and adherence to a budget, the Atlanta housewife saved money and earned 15 minutes of fame in the process.

After an Atlanta newspaper published a story about her, *Life* magazine ran a feature on Ann's uncanny budgeting prowess in November 1947 (see photo below). Then the wife of high school teacher Hamilton Williams, Ann fed a family of four (plus a cat) on a mere $12.50 a week, recalls her daughter Kappy Bowers of Lithonia, Georgia.

Along with scanning grocery store advertisements in papers and promotions in store windows, Ann accomplished this feat by eliminating meat for lunches and serving entrees like hamburgers, meat loaf and chili.

"Back then, teachers barely made enough to live on," Kappy says. "Mom tackled problems full speed ahead. So if she was going to save money, she was going to save as much as she could."

Being a budget queen required discipline and time—and some comfortable shoes.

"It took a lot of time to make out menus for the week, then ferret out the good deals by hitting two or three grocery stores during weekly shopping trips," Kappy says.

Kappy says her mother, who passed away in 2011, was very proud to be featured in *Life*.

"She was not a shrinking violet," she says. "She wasn't showy, but she was proud of what she was

doing, and happy to participate. Her only surprise was that some didn't think it was so wonderful."

Kappy's mother received some disparaging letters from other housewives around the country whose husbands were pressuring them to work the same budgetary magic in their homes.

"We just laughed at those letters," Kappy says.

As time went on, Ann—who had earned a chemistry degree in college—went back to school to get a master's in education and became a kindergarten teacher.

"Back then, they wouldn't hire

women for jobs in chemistry," Kappy says. "So she got a teaching degree. After she became a full-time teacher, she was a little less frugal because she didn't have the time to go to such extremes.

"But Mom loved a good deal and shopped at discount stores. She was always looking for a bargain and loved to call to tell me about the latest deal she found. She taught us that the first thing you do in a store is head for the sale shelves. It was a long time before I ever bought anything that wasn't on sale. Her frugalness made a strong impression on me."

STITCH IN TIME "This photo from, I think, the late 1930s shows the Kinsley, Kansas, ladies' sewing circle on the third floor of the Edwards County Courthouse," writes Bob Smith of Nickerson. His grandmothers are Grace Duncan-Cox (third from left in front) and Eva Ann Kennedy-Smith (to the right of her, with eyeglasses).

BEST CHRISTMAS
"This photo from 1940 is my favorite," says Margaret Street of Pleasant Grove, Alabama. "It was a good year, as the war hadn't started. I'm the youngest (right), sitting with my brother, Henry, and sister, Elsie. Every Christmas, a relative took our picture and gave us a copy as a memento. This custom began in 1932 and ended when my brother went into the Navy in 1945. We're still a close family, although we live in different cities now. As we look back, we realize this was one of the best years of our lives."

1940

CHAPTER 7

Let's Celebrate

❖

Some of the richest deposits in our memory banks are made
during holidays and special occasions. They are times
for generations to gather, tell stories, take pictures and
capture a multitude of heartwarming moments.

Red-Letter Occasions
SIMPLE NOTES SPARK A FLOOD OF MEMORIES

"PUPPY LOVE" WAS TENDER AND TENSE

I was pleasantly surprised when one of my grade-school classmates dropped me a letter. She'd read some of my recollections in *Reminisce* and wanted to share a memory of her own from the 1930s.

She reminded me that I had presented her with a Hershey bar after she'd been away from class for a funeral. I guess we were in fifth grade at the time.

Back then, a boy would have to be seriously in love to give a girl a Hershey bar…and I was. But I was too shy to do much more than worship her from afar—and sacrifice a Hershey bar at the altar of devotion.

I did persuade Mom and Dad to join the Lutheran church just so I could be in the youth groups she belonged to. But never could I build up the courage to ask her for a date. If she turned me down, my life would be over. That's puppy love for you.

Kids today still have crushes, but all the rules have changed…and not for the better. In my day, for example, girls never called boys on the telephone. Instead, they waited (and waited) for the boy of their dreams to call them.

The only chances for overt displays of interest came on Valentine's Day and May Day. On Valentine's Day, kids swapped cards at school, dumping them into a big cardboard box the teacher brought for the occasion. (I always felt sorry for those classmates who got only a few valentines.)

For me, the real moment of crisis came at Hallett's Books and Stationery store, where I picked out the valentines. I'd search and search for a card to send to the one classmate I was especially interested in.

It was a tricky piece of diplomacy—I wanted her to know I thought she was special, but I didn't dare choose a card that was too gushy.

After Valentine's Day, the next big sweethearts' occasion was May Day. Dad always used to say that

the sap flowed in spring—in boys as well as in trees and shrubs. I was as sappy as the next guy.

Remember May baskets? All winter, Mom saved cylindrical Quaker Oats boxes, which, cut in half, became two May baskets. My sister and I covered our baskets with crepe paper, attached a pipe-cleaner handle wrapped with more crepe paper, then filled each basket with goodies such as popcorn and jelly beans.

It was easy to pick out the baskets I'd made—they looked as if they'd been run over by a car soon after they were put together. The crepe paper was rumpled and uglified with gooey smears of flour-and-water paste, and the handle was twisted and bent, as though afflicted with an advanced case of arthritis.

My sister's baskets, meanwhile, were flawless and looked…well, as if a girl had made them.

On the big day, Mom or Dad would drive us from house to house with a car full of May baskets. We'd run up to the front porch, deposit a May basket, ring

the bell and run back to the car.

Driving away, we'd peer back in the hope of seeing the object of our affection step outside to pick up our offering. (I've often wondered if the guy who started United Parcel Service got the idea from delivering May baskets.)

As with the valentines, there was always one May basket that was intended for the special person in your heart. It may have had a few more crepe-paper ruffles on it or an extra dozen jelly beans or a sprig of forsythia to make it different.

Another more permanent way to show affection was to carve hearts and initials on trees. However, once word got around that you were sweet on someone, you risked the shame of having classmates chalk phrases like "Jimmy Loves Janice" on every sidewalk around school. All you could do then was pray for rain.

Years ago, childhood romances may have simmered with the same intensity as they seem to today. But kids were on a much shorter leash with strict parent-

imposed curfews, fewer cars, and neighbors who knew one another and cared about each other.

Fathers had a secret stopwatch in their heads that kicked in when you brought their daughters home from a date. If your fond farewells on the front porch ran too long, the porch light suddenly came on and her dad peered through the little glass window in the front door.

When it came to curfews, most kids tried to stretch things a bit. My family lived on a gravel road where the lights of every approaching car shone right in my parents' bedroom window.

On nights when I returned home past curfew, I'd speed up our '39 Plymouth, flick off the headlights, put the car in neutral, turn off the motor and attempt to coast all the way to the garage.

I became remarkably good at it, considering I had to negotiate the turn into our lane without throwing gravel or running up onto the lawn. I was the original Stealth bomber!

Small towns created particular obstacles to romance—there was always the issue of who you liked versus who your mother thought you should like. Rarely was there a match—puppy love is blissfully resistant to family feuds or friendships.

Still, the slower pace of romance back then had lasting dividends. A neighboring boy and girl became fond of each other when they were 8 years old, and they're obviously still quite fond of each other today, considerably more than a half-century later.

Young love is a wonderful, perplexing, sleep-robbing, all-consuming, sweaty-palms, heart-pounding, totally irrational part of growing up. I wouldn't have missed it for anything—nor would I ever want to go through it again. I know…I was there.

CLANCY STROCK
CONTRIBUTING EDITOR

LASTING LABOR OF LOVE

A tiny note was found in my mother-in-law's wallet when she died in 1982. The message had been scrawled out by my husband, James Wright, when he was 8 years old, in 1932.

The Depression was raging that year, and the Wright family had chosen to move from their big home in Birmingham, Alabama, to their country house. Times were hard, but the children were just happy to be near their dear grandparents.

On the Saturday before Mother's Day, all the children at breakfast were excited except Jimmie, who was very worried.

Dad was taking the children into town that morning to get gifts for Mother, but Jimmie had forgotten about it the previous day, when he had agreed to clear the weeds behind the house of Paw-Paw, his grandfather.

Jimmie, who was very serious for an 8-year-old and wanted very much to be a grown man, couldn't go back on his word to Paw-Paw. He decided that if he worked hard enough, he could finish the job by noon and make the trip.

As Jimmie rushed to chop down all those weeds, the lot seemed to grow bigger and the sun got hotter. He hardly heard Dad call out that it was time to go, and he wistfully waved goodbye and turned back to his job.

Next, Jimmie raked all the weeds into a big pile and burned them. By the end of the day, he was exhausted, but also very proud. The field of weeds was now a beautifully cleared piece of farmland.

Paw-Paw could hardly believe his eyes when he came out to pay Jimmie for the job. From his purse, he handed Jimmie the two dimes they had agreed on.

Jimmie raced home to tell Mother how pleased Paw-Paw was. Just as he dashed into the house, he heard his sisters and brothers excitedly telling Mother about the gift they could hardly wait to give her.

As Mother looked across the room, she saw Jimmie standing there, so hot and tired, dirty and sunburned. Suddenly, his big brown eyes filled with tears, and Mother saw him struggle to hold them back because Dad had told him that a man doesn't cry.

That night, Mother heard Jimmie up long after he had gone to bed and wondered what he could be doing.

The next morning, Mother found the answer by her plate at the breakfast table. It was a tiny piece of blue paper, and as she unfolded it, two shiny dimes fell out onto the table.

Mother could hardly read the note as her eyes filled with tears. It was a rhyme that read, "I worked as hard as work could be till I turned as red as a beet, To make a little bit of pay to give to you on Mother's day. from Jimmie"

Fifty years later, the very same dimes were being carried with that little note, kept all that time by Mother.

MARY ANNE WRIGHT OCEAN HILLS, CA

GREAT AND SMALL
The author's husband (shown above in 1932) saw two dimes and a short poem as small gifts, but they proved to be quite large in his mother's eyes.

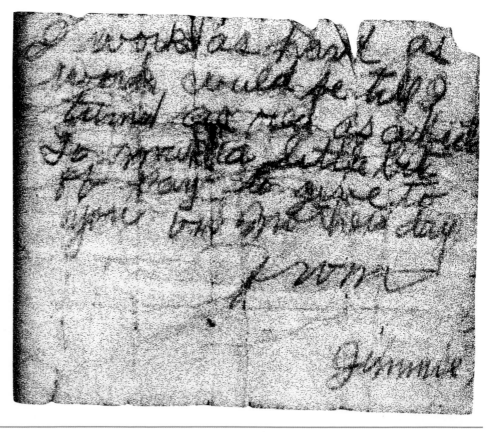

REFLECTIONS OF MOTHER "This is my favorite picture of my mother, Edna Wissman," says Susan Patrick of Muskegon, Michigan. "It was taken at home, in Grand Rapids, Michigan, in 1945. Mother was home with her first child, my sister Karen, who was about 18 months old then; I was next in line. Here, Mother was waiting for our father, Robert, who was in the Marine Corps, to come home from World War II."

Easter Parade

THIS HOLIDAY PUTS A SPRING IN EVERYONE'S STEP

OLD RED SEIZED THE DAY

My brother Gary called our dad's theories on life "farmer's economics." Everything except the basics should go for crops and livestock—money was the only motivator.

And so it was that Dad figured the only way to get his teen and preteen boys interested in the annual Easter egg hunt back home in Shreveport, Louisiana, was to make it financially rewarding.

He took a crayon and wrote "$1" on all but one of the eggs. That last egg was to be the jackpot and had "$5" written on it.

There was no whining from us

about being too old for the hunt! The possibility of finding five or six $1 eggs and putting them with the $5 egg was more than enough for us! After all, those rewards would pay for a movie date or a new model airplane.

So come Easter morning, we moved with a purpose, running from one time-tested hiding place to another. It often got physical, and Dad liked that part of it.

The tall grass that grew over the septic tank was the likely hiding spot, and when two of us got there at the same time, there was a lot of hip blocking to knock a brother past the grass while you hit the ground for the egg.

These were moves one didn't see at the Easter egg hunt on the church grounds.

Old Red, our dog, loved our roughhousing as much as we did, and he got excited with all the running. He'd sometimes grab our jeans, although he didn't know what was happening. (That's us in the photo with Old Red. From left there's Steve, Gary and me.)

The most memorable hunt was in 1964, when I came home from college. After the normal flurry of activity, our dad took an inventory to make sure we had found all the eggs. He did not want a rotting leftover stinking up the yard when the lawn mower hit it.

There was one egg still not found—the jackpot egg. Dad told us the general area where he thought it was, and the search continued until brothers Steve and Gary spotted the egg in a weedy area along the creek by the back fence.

They both broke for the egg, followed closely by Old Red at full speed. But they were too quick, and the egg was no sooner grabbed than it was dropped and broken.

That was fine with Old Red, who promptly ate the egg and most of the shell.

But there was enough of the shell to verify that it was the $5 egg, so both Steve and Gary declared their claim on the prize.

Dad disagreed, saying neither brother had control. The prize would go to Old Red. Sure enough, on Monday, Old Red had a brand-new $5 bed where his old blanket used to be.

DAN COYLE HIGHLAND VILLAGE, TX

"HOPPY" FASHION SHOW In 1949, Dyla Greenlaw (front row center) and friends (clockwise: Marilyn Roberts, Carolyn Jones, Gwendolyn Knights, Donna Wheelock and Nancy Smith) were bunnies in a fashion show in Waterville, Maine. "My aunt Gwendolyn Foster (in dress) sang 'Easter Parade' as each bunny escorted a model down the runway," Dyla writes from Yemassee, South Carolina.

SO EXCITED There's no doubt Roxie Kump was happy on Easter 1965. "She was thrilled with her basket," writes her mother, Joan, of Aspers, Pennsylvania.

SWEET AUNT "My aunt Penelope Sweeney was a decorator at the Heidelberg Candy factory in Philadelphia, Pennsylvania," says Richard Barron of Tampa, Florida. "She's on the left in this 1949 photo. On Easter morning, my brothers and I were each given our own 2½-pound chocolate egg, which she had decorated with our names!"

Patriotic Pride

Celebrating the red, white and blue is a joy for these happy readers. Take a peek into their scrapbook as they share their favorite Independence Day photos with you.

◄ THIS FLAG IS ON THE MOVE

These young women in Crete, Nebraska, must have done quite a bit of extra sewing in 1923 to come up with this living tribute to Old Glory. Bernice Sanderson, now of Los Angeles, was one of the "stripe girls" (she's second from the right).

LET FREEDOM RING ►

"My stepfather, Harry Davidson, took this photo of the Liberty Bell when it came through Ogden, Utah, in 1915 on its way to the Panama-Pacific International Exposition in San Francisco," says Mollie Weldon of Shreveport, Louisiana. "Harry says there was a walkway around the bell on its flatcar, so people who came to see the bell could walk up and actually touch it."

◄ **SISTERS SALUTE**

"I was 4 and my sister, Barb (right), was 5 when this picture was taken in Rochester, New York, by our mom, Gloria Northrup, on July 4, 1960," writes Jean Yates of Churchville, New York. "We lived with our grandmother Helen Figler until 1962, when we moved two doors down. What great memories we share of those lovely days spent together!"

▲ **AMERICA SOARS!**

"The Fourth of July parade in Sharonville, Ohio, with its bicycle contestants, drew the imagination of my children, Brad (left) and Bill Lamb," says Elizabeth Lamb of Albany, Oregon. "Every year, we'd have a family conference on what best represented the occasion. Once, it was the five flags that have flown over Ohio. Another time, it was the three Revolutionary soldiers from the famous painting. Above, in 1969, America was about to put men on the moon."

Fall Festivities

RUFFLED FEATHERS

My husband's company had given each employee a live turkey for Thanksgiving. As a young wife and mother, I had limited cooking skills that certainly didn't include preparing any food that ate corn and gobbled!

I couldn't face putting the bird on the chopping block, as I had seen my father do on Thanksgivings past. So, with my infant son lying on a pillow on the front seat beside me and the live turkey on the backseat—tied in a sack with its head sticking out—I drove our old Chrysler Airflow toward a downtown market to have the bird prepared.

Charlotte, North Carolina, was a city of tall buildings, noisy traffic, confusing lights and signs, and crowds of people scurrying about. All these activities were intimidating to an inexperienced driver unfamiliar with the city.

My concentration was shattered by the sound of a piercing whistle. I slowed and looked out to see a Goliath-sized policeman motioning for me to pull over.

For a moment, I could see myself in jail, sitting on a cold cot, baby and turkey beside me, having a skimpy Thanksgiving dinner on a greasy tray.

As the officer approached, he rumbled loudly, "Young lady, this is a one-way street, and you're going the wrong way!"

With two giant hands on the door, he stuck his head inside. Suddenly, the turkey let out a loud gobble, awakening the baby, who cried uncontrollably. My own tears cascaded like Niagara Falls.

The officer pushed his cap

BABY BERT Hubert Tish Jr. is pictured with his mother, Lottie, around the time of the turkey incident.

back, scratched his head and, with a big grin, said, "Well, I can see you've got plenty of problems without me giving you a ticket."

He held back traffic and gave me a signal to turn around and head in the opposite direction. I did, and went straight home!

Once there, our neighbor helped me get the turkey out of the car and into the garage.

When my husband came home that day, I told him of the whole ordeal. To my chagrin, he responded by laughing.

"Since you think it's so funny,

you take care of the turkey," I said. "I'm not having anything else to do with that bird!" With a hug, he promised to have the bird ready for Thanksgiving.

Thanksgiving Day dawned dark, and it began to rain, then sleet. We put the turkey in a roaster on the flat top of the woodstove that heated the house. All day, the turkey cooked as its appetizing aroma filled every room.

We ate by candlelight very late that night, but it was a Thanksgiving we never forgot.
LOTTIE TISH TALLAHASSEE, FL

▲ TRIO WITH A COMMON THREAD

"My wife, Bette, sewed all three of these Halloween outfits for our children (from left), Lori as Raggedy Ann, Jeff as Raggedy Andy and Linda as Little Red Riding Hood," says Charlie VanderMeer of Grand Rapids, Michigan. The picture was taken in 1965 as they prepared to go trick-or-treating.

Making Merry

CHRISTMAS BRINGS OUT THE FINEST IN EVERYONE

SCHOOL TUNED IN TO SANTA'S VISIT

The most dramatic event of the 1937 school year for the one-room Viola Villa School was Santa's arrival.

I taught school for two years at the school, located near my childhood home in Phillips, Wisconsin. At 19, I held a responsible position. More important in 1937, I had an income of $75 a month—nothing to be sneezed at.

During my first winter as a teacher, I brought in a radio and placed it on a table in the center of the stage before the packed house at the annual Christmas program.

Unknown to the audience, my brother, Wilmar, was in a closet with a microphone and a car battery. The mike was a new gimmick at the time. When a switch was pushed, it would cut out the radio program and allow him to speak through the radio.

At the end of the program, I announced I would try to get a report from Santa Claus, then turned the dial as we heard several radio stations.

Wilmar cut in on his mike and said, "Ho, ho, ho. This is Santa Claus, and I'm on my way to the Viola Villa School." He then described the blizzard he had to go through and the difficulty he had in staying on course to find the tiny country school.

By the second time he mentioned the school by name, you could have heard a pin drop in the audience. Parents, students and their older brothers and sisters knew such a thing was impossible, yet they were hearing Santa Claus on the radio!

When Santa said he spotted the school and was heading his sleigh for the schoolyard, several people actually got up and looked out the windows.

The man we had lined up to play Santa was in on the deal, too. He came in, ho-ho-ho-ing and stomping through the door, then repeated the things my brother had said on the radio about the blizzard and finding the school. The whole thing was pulled off beautifully.

The incident remained memorable for those involved: Seventeen years afterward, Joe Rehak, one of my sixth-grade students at Viola Villa, wrote an essay while working on his college degree. He titled it "The Unforgettable Mr. Glissendorf" and mentioned Santa and the radio.

I'm 84 at this writing and I'm still basking in the warm memories of my years as a country teacher.
OWEN GLISSENDORF URBANA, IL

UNFORGETTABLE Joe Rehak (with wife, above) recalled Santa's report and visit. That's Owen at the school building, now the town hall.

THE STORY BEHIND
THE CHRISTMAS ROCKER

The newspaper ad I'd placed read, "Wanted to Buy: Old Comfortable Rocking Chair."

My ad was answered and an address was given. A small woman, her white hair drawn into a tight bun at the nape of her neck, opened the door.

She ushered me into her old-fashioned living room but avoided my questions about the rocker. Instead she asked about my plans, my interests and how I felt about old furniture.

After what seemed like a long time, the old woman became silent. Then she cleared her throat and began to tell me this story:

"When I was a little girl, around 1903, my family lived on a farm near Carthage. We were poor but happy, and the weeks before Christmas were spent preparing food and each hiding our handmade gifts to be exchanged.

"On Christmas morning, everyone had a gift—except my father had not given Mother a present. As she tried to hide her disappointment, Dad donned his winter hat and coat and started through the snowy yard toward the barn.

"Morning chores were over, but Dad did not return to the house. Wiping the frost from the windows, we looked eagerly across the fields, but he was nowhere to be seen.

"Then my brother, his nose pressed against the windowpane, called out, 'I see Dad coming from the neighbors' house—and he's carrying something on his shoulders!'

"The large object he was hauling became larger as he approached. Then Dad stepped into the kitchen and unwrapped the most beautiful oak rocking chair I had ever seen. This was his gift to Mother.

"After harvest, he had ordered it from our new 1903 Sears, Roebuck catalog. A wagon delivered it to our neighbor's house, where it was lovingly wrapped and stored for the autumn in their barn.

"Mom gently touched the rocker, moved it close to our wood-burning stove, sat down and gently began to rock. This gift of Father's was a loved and cherished Christmas present.

"Mom spent many hours sitting beside the stove, rocking and enjoying the aroma of baking bread."

The woman then turned to study me. "I'm all that's left of my family," she continued. "They've all died and I have no one to care for my rocker. It must go to someone who will love, cherish and keep it always."

I paid for the rocker and carefully loaded it into my pickup. As I drove away, I could see the woman watching from the doorway. Touched by her story, I drove to my dad's house to talk.

I repeated the story and could see that he, too, was touched. "Leave it here," he said, "and I'll glue the joints for you."

For the next few years, every time I visited Dad, he was sitting and rocking in that old chair. Now his favorite pastimes of reading and rocking were combined. Not a word was ever mentioned about returning the rocker to me, and I was perfectly fine with that.

Years later, after Dad passed away, that golden oak rocker came back to me. With its arms worn smooth by the touch of loving hands, it now sits in my living room (above).

Each year at Christmas after I decorate my tree, I sit in the rocker and think of a snowy morning in 1903 and a loving father's gift, and of my own dad.

I cherish that lovely Christmas rocker and will make sure its story lives on when someday it is passed on to the person chosen as its next owner.

JUDI WEBER CARTHAGE, MO

WATCH THE TREE ➤

David Button awaits a pass from his dad as the two hold a little impromptu indoor football scrimmage on Christmas morning in the late '50s or early '60s. Sister Mindy appears to be waiting to see where the ball lands before she gets back to her present–a more ladylike fashion designer set. The children's dad, David, sent the slide from Artesia, New Mexico.

◀ PLAYING HER PLATTERS

"My brother, Ed Born, and I never slept Christmas Eve, anticipating the next day's surprises," writes Patti Monahan from Tucson, Arizona. She is shown with her phono and 78-rpm records in Jamaica, New York, in 1952.

▲ ON DANCER

Those aren't really reindeer above, explains Anne Curfman of Hampton, Virginia. She should know...she's the little girl standing next to the sleigh in this 1935 picture. A friend of her family in Tidewater, Virginia, constructed the sleigh and antlers for his goats.

➤ CHRISTMAS PAST AND PRESENT

1957 was a good one for the Clifford family. "That's when my sister Jacque received a saxophone and my brother Fred got a set of barbells," writes Jean Pupeter from Janesville, Wisconsin. "I took this photo with my new Christmas camera! Our gifts were never wrapped. They were just neatly arranged under the tree." Living in Appleton, Wisconsin, at the time, the family rented part of their house to a young social worker named Lois Picklemeier. "She was such a wonderful person that I decided on social work for my career, too," says Jean.

Reader Favorites

HER HOLIDAY WAS MERRY AND BRIGHT

PRESENT CAME AS A SHOCK

Our family of 10 was still feeling the Depression in northern Minnesota in 1947. We fared better than some in town who didn't have gardens. But they had two things we lacked—electricity and running water.

Our house was paid for when we married in 1935, but it was small and we hadn't figured on such a big family.

Washing clothes for 10 people, three of them babies, with no running water was a backbreaking job. I used a gas-powered washing machine, which was all right in the summer, but in colder weather, I couldn't bring the machine into the house because it smoked so much. I had to resort to the scrub board.

I did have an electric washing machine, but all I could do was look at it, as there was no electricity in our area yet.

That summer, workers for the Rural Electrification Administration (REA) arrived. You can imagine the excitement when crews set the poles. Another crew came in the fall and strung the wires. We were all set—or so we thought.

Thanksgiving came and went; still no electricity. Our house had some wiring, but nothing was connected to the poles outside.

The day before Christmas, I was doing last-minute baking and preparing for the holiday. All I could anticipate was the large volume of wash awaiting me. The babies were out of clean nighties and diapers.

I was about to make a phone call when it rang. We were on a

POLE SITTERS The author's children posed around the utility pole three years after electricity came to their house in Minnesota.

party line, and I took the receiver off the hook in time to hear a neighbor tell her sister, "They just left here and I turned on all the lights. My, it looks fine!"

I broke in, "Christine, what are you talking about? The lights?"

"Yes," she said, "and they're coming your way! They should be there in half an hour."

"Thanks," I said, and hung up. "Kids!" I shouted. "Get on your duds and start carrying water."

I pushed the Christmas pudding to the back burner and put the wash boiler on the front of the stove. I stoked the fire as the kids brought the water.

In a half-hour, the REA truck pulled into the yard. I watched, eagerly, as a spry man jumped out, climbed the pole in the

yard and turned on the juice!

"Santa Claus," I said to myself.

Fifteen minutes later, the new electric washing machine was happily swishing a load of clothes, and everyone stood around in awe.

Before supper, all the washing was done and clothes were hanging to dry wherever there was room. I finally plopped down on the couch, exhausted but oh-so happy.

Santa might have had a hard time finding the stockings waiting for him that night, as they were hidden by the drying clothes, but I don't think he minded.

As for me, the gift of electricity was the best Christmas present I ever received.

ALVERNA ANDERSON BIG FORK, MN

AT BEDTIME Stories were the way the Fenno family ended the day back in 1953. Howard Fenno of Wichita, Kansas, sent in this photo of his wife, Esther, reading a Christmas story to daughter Debra, 9 months, and son Gail, 3, in the bedroom of their Lafayette, Indiana, home. Merry Christmas to all...and to all a good night!

OPENING WEEK On the morning of May 27, 1937, the city of San Francisco was buzzing. After four years of construction, the Golden Gate Bridge—the longest and tallest suspension bridge in the world—was open for business. Pedestrian Day kicked off the weeklong Golden Gate Bridge Fiesta, and as many as 300,000 walkers, runners, bicyclists, unicyclists, tap dancers and even stilt-walkers paid 25 cents apiece to cross the span. At noon the following day, President Franklin Roosevelt tapped a telegraph key in the White House, declaring the Golden Gate open to traffic. By midnight, some 32,300 cars had crossed the bridge.

CHAPTER 8

Come Along
For the Ride

Ready for a good old-fashioned road trip? We've saved you
a seat in some pretty classy vehicles, revved up for a
freewheeling journey into the past. Buckle your seat belt,
and remember that getting there is half the fun!

Motoring Memories

IT'S ALL RELATIVE WHEN IT COMES TO REMINISCING

LITTLE RED CORVETTE

One spring afternoon in 1957 in Cleveland, Ohio, my sister Patricia and I turned the corner on our walk home to see a sleek sports car parked in our driveway. We thought someone must be visiting.

"Whose car?" we excitedly asked our parents.

"Ours!" my father replied, walking toward us with a broad grin lighting up his face. My mother stood riveted near the garage. She didn't seem happy.

"It's a Chevrolet Corvette," he added. "Lipstick-red convertible, whitewall tires and a hard top for rainy days." (See photo below.) Dad looked the way he did when our brother was born.

"Don't forget, it seats only two," Mother chimed in. "But that's OK. We'll just go places in shifts."

My father avoided looking at her and asked, "Want to go for a ride?"

We all piled in and took off down the street. My mother sat in the passenger seat holding my baby brother, Dale, and my middle sister, Patricia, on her lap. My oldest sister, Cheryl, huddled on the floor next to Mom's legs, and I was wedged in the opening behind the gearshift.

"Well, this is certainly comfortable," my mother said.

A red plaid cap appeared on my father's head. We knew without being told that it was a racing cap. Whenever Dad did something, he did it all the way.

My dad lived his life at full throttle, pedal to the metal, not slowing down for the curves. He golfed, hunted, skied, fished, flew airplanes, did archery, rode motorcycles and raced hydroplanes, as well as go-carts and anything else with wheels.

As an infantry soldier, my father survived some of the deadliest battles of World War II and was sent home with a scar across his forehead, where a bullet had nearly killed him. He then spent 30 years putting out fires and saving lives as a firefighter.

Whatever it was that gave him his courage also instilled in him a dedication to duty and family. He always had two jobs and never missed a day of work. He even trudged 15 miles to the firehouse after 29 inches of snow virtually shut down the city on Thanksgiving 1950. Forty-eight hours later, he walked back home.

In the end, my mother came to terms with my father's need to speed around town in his snazzy new car. Her resignation was helped along by an Autumn Haze mink stole with her initials embroidered in large gold letters on the silk lining—Dad's reparation for his impulse purchase. (She's wearing the stole in the photo below along with, from left, me and my sisters Patricia and Cheryl.)

Our parents are gone now, as is the Corvette—traded in for a wood-paneled station wagon. We fondly recall that time in Cleveland when the days seemed longer and the problems smaller.

It makes us happy to know that amid the hardships of raising four children, there were many special evenings when Mother, her mink draped over her shoulders, slid into the Corvette next to my father, and they sped down the road in the moonlight.

SUZIE DAVIDSON
SAN DIEGO, CA

WELCOMING COMMITTEE
Dock Coffey (left) provided the Pontiac, and Betty Smith Davis (center) and her friend Faye Hill provided the welcome to new neighbors in Amarillo.

HOWDY, NEIGHBOR

I remember the flashy new Pontiac used by my mom, Betty Smith Davis, for the local Hi-Neighbor program in 1953. Dock Coffey Pontiac and other merchants in Amarillo, Texas, launched the innovative service to welcome new residents.

For a few hours a day, Mom and her friend Faye Hill encouraged other businesses to initiate sponsorships with gifts such as discount coupons. Mom remembers they had to fill the Pontiac's tank with gas, but the use of the car was invaluable because Dad traveled, leaving Mom without transportation.

Mom says she cherishes the confidence she developed through an opportunity few women were afforded in the '50s.
CAROLYN DAVIS BARKER CANYON, TX

STOP THE PRESSES! "My uncle Amasa Howe was a reporter for the *Boston Globe* during the '30s and '40s," writes Frederic Howe of Falmouth, Maine. "This photo was taken in 1946. My uncle was the first newspaper reporter in New England to have a car radio-telephone, which was a 'sensational advance in the history of communications.' When Amasa passed away, the Boston Newspaper Guild established an award in his memory."

THE GAS, NOT THE GALS "Above is a photo of me and my sisters in 1938 in Parker, South Dakota," says Dorothy Veverka (standing in back) of Jackson, Minnesota. "My sisters are, from left, Lucille, Mary, Bertha, Marguerite and Agnes. With the high price of gas today, I thought the picture was very interesting."

MEMORIES ON THREE WHEELS

In the late '40s, I lived with my mother in Hollywood, California. My mother was a photographic retoucher and color artist and worked at home for several of the photo studios.

One day a photographer who brought some work to my mother asked me if I wanted a modeling job posing with the Davis three-wheel car. I had done a little modeling, so I agreed.

Local newscaster Clete Roberts drove the photographer, another woman and me to an area along Mulholland Drive, where the photos, including this one (above), were taken.

A couple of months later, the photographer called to tell me my picture was in the January 1947 issue of an automotive magazine. I then called the Davis Motorcar Co. to ask about my modeling fee.

I was invited to the plant, got a short tour, signed a release and collected a check for $10, which wasn't bad pay in those days.

I didn't drive the car and didn't ask to, as I hadn't driven a car. I often wondered what would have happened if the front tire blew!

After I was married, my husband and I, and later our two children, lived in a house three blocks from the Davis facility.

ANITA LIEN SMITH CANYON LAKE, CA

BOSS FUELED A SECRET, BUT NOW IT'S REVEALED

This photo was taken on the last day I ever pumped gas from McCurdy's Atlantic Service in Altoona, Pennsylvania. It was Nov. 6, 1940, and the building was demolished that day. Mr. Louse, the man whose car I'm filling, was a longtime customer.

There was a secret about the building behind us. Not only did it serve as the office, but it was the gasoline storage and pumping station. At the top of the building was a large tank that was filled with water. Under the building was a gasoline storage tank.

The water was fed through a pipe into the gasoline tank. After 15 minutes, the water and gasoline separated, with the water on the bottom. The water pressure pushed the gasoline into pumps.

In those days, a lot of filling stations had trouble with water in their gasoline. We did not. In fact, we guaranteed there was no water in our gas. Still, my boss told me to never tell anyone how our pumping system worked. He was afraid people wouldn't buy from him if they knew.

This photo marked the end of that system, since the building was replaced with a modern station and electric pumps.

JOHN KEHOE JR. LOCKPORT, NY

CABBIE HAD IT COVERED

This photo of me was taken in 1963, when I worked as a driver for the Red Cab Co. In Toledo, Ohio. The picture, which includes our secretary Millie, appeared on a magazine cover for the *Ohio Bell Voice*.

Back then, a driver would get out of the cab and open the door for the customer before collecting the fare. Drivers made change from the coin changers attached to their belts, always hoping for tips but not always receiving them.

Cab drivers worked 10 hours a day, six days a week, and take-home pay was about $42, with maybe an additional $5 in tips. But it was enough for me to get married to a beautiful gal named Ginnie, and we've had a long and happy marriage.

Red Cab was my first job in a lengthy career of driving, mostly in semis. Since I retired, I have driven school buses in Toledo. Driving has been a wonderful career, and I wouldn't trade it, or Ginnie, for the world.

LUCKEY PENN TOLEDO, OH

WHEN RUMBLE SEATS RULED

In 1932, my boyfriend (now my husband) bought a car with a rumble seat. Oh, how I remember that roadster! We enjoyed dating in that car but never got a chance to take a romantic ride in the rumble seat until the day a new bridge opened. That bridge joined our hometown of Evansville, Indiana, with Henderson, Kentucky. Of course, everyone in both towns wanted to cross it. We asked our friends George and Virginia to go to the opening ceremony. But there was one condition: We asked George to drive so Fred and I could sit in the rumble seat for the first time. They agreed, and we got into a long line waiting to cross. It took over two hours, and we both got a bad case of sunburn. But as you can see in the photograph, the big kiss I got made it all worthwhile.

ESTHER LOGE EVANSVILLE, IN

REFLECTIVE "When our son, Rocky, was 17 months old, we took this slide of him in Sulphur, Oklahoma, in September 1950," write Roy and Carrie Jane Miller of Oklahoma City. "Those were the days of real white sidewall tires, not the skinny things you see today."

A Dream on Wheels

AUTOMOBILES FUELED THEIR STORIES FOR YEARS

HIS OWN PRIVATE JET

In September 1965, textbook salesman Homer Williams became a minor celebrity in Tulsa, Oklahoma—sort of a down-home combination of Chuck Yeager and George Jetson. That's what happens when you're one of 203 people nationwide selected to take Chrysler's futuristic jet engine car for a three-month test drive.

Hailed as the next big thing in automobiles, the sleek car in shiny Turbine Bronze attracted attention wherever Williams drove it. In fact, the day after the Williams family took delivery amid much media fanfare at a nearby Holiday Inn, a local minister almost preached to empty pews, says the late Williams' son, Randy, who still lives in Tulsa.

"We lived next door to a church that my family attended, and the car was parked out in the driveway on that Sunday morning," he says. "People knew Dad had the car because local TV stations had broadcast the story. So many people walked over to look at it that the minister had to come and gather his flock for church."

The car's allure was no surprise, says Steve Lehto, author of *Chrysler's Turbine Car: The Rise and Fall of Detroit's Coolest Creation.*

"In the mid-1950s, we were in the space race with the Russians, and technological advancements occurred at a breakneck pace," he said in an interview. "Rockets put satellites into space, and jetliners were shrinking the globe. It was only a matter of time before someone put a jet engine in a car. Chrysler stylists were clearly playing to the public's fascination with space."

At the time Homer Williams started his love affair with the Turbine Car, 189 people from all walks of life, living in 48 states and the District of Columbia, had already logged more than 900,000 miles of Turbine driving, according to documents supplied by Williams' grandson, Michael Oakes. The program marked the first time any major U.S. auto manufacturer had tried such a hands-on evaluation. Chrysler Corp. officials selected the drivers from more than 30,000 people who'd written unsolicited letters asking to take the car for a spin.

In a television interview years later, Williams cops to exceeding the speed limit. Just a little. "At one time I did get carried away," he says in the interview.

"I was on the turnpike going to Wichita, and I said, 'OK, it looks clear.' I started revving it up, and when I reached 120, I decided that was fast enough."

Randy says he drove the car, too—albeit with his father's hand on the steering wheel.

"Shortly before we had to turn it back in, Dad got me behind the wheel on a new highway near our house," he recalls. "It was quite a thrill, especially with that jet engine sound."

The car always drew admirers wherever Williams went, whether he was stopped at a red light or parked at high schools and college campuses in Oklahoma and Kansas, his sales territory.

"He developed a spiel about the car—what it ran on, the number of moving parts and so forth," says Randy. "When he was finished, he'd start the car with the hood and doors open and demonstrate how smooth it ran by standing a nickel on edge atop the engine's air intake cover. He would've been a great salesman for Chrysler."

Williams was crazy about the car, as evidenced by letters he sent to Chrysler during the testing period. "I feel sure the Chrysler Turbine Car is destined for a great future and may well revolutionize the automobile industry."

Alas, that was not to be. But Williams might have found comfort to learn the car he reluctantly gave back to Chrysler in 1965 is one of the few turbine car prototypes Chrysler didn't destroy. Its current owner is another celebrity: one Jay Leno, onetime *Tonight Show* host and car collector extraordinaire.

◄ A STICK-Y SITUATION

"I bumped into a few tombstones in 1948 when my patient father taught me to drive a stick shift in a cemetery," says Betsy Leacock of Tucson, Arizona. "It took a while to get the hang of it, but to get a license then, you had to drive a manual transmission. It all paid off later when Dad bought a new 1951 Studebaker. I loved to drive the nifty car with its distinctive bullet nose and grille. That's me with the car, and my mom standing behind me."

THE RETURN OF RED FEATHER

It was love at first sight when I walked into the showroom on a spring day in 1960 and saw this 1957 Chevrolet Bel Air (above and at right). I had been working and saving for a new car for almost a year since high school graduation.

There were about a half-dozen teenage boys hanging around when I went into the office to close the deal. I heard them muttering about how a car like that would be "wasted on a girl."

The next day, I took my grandmother for a ride. She was impressed with the way the car seemed to float along the road, just like a red feather. The name stuck, and from then on, my car was Red Feather.

Years passed. I got married, and we decided to sell the car. I hated to, but it was the practical thing to do.

I had forgotten about the car until the day my husband came home and said, "I think I found that old car of yours. It's behind a garage in a small town not far from here."

We went to see the car, and I instantly knew it was Red Feather! The owner sold the car to us, and after lots of time and money, including another '57 Chevy for parts, Red Feather was wonderfully restored to its former glory.

We eventually sold Red Feather again, but I'll always treasure the miles we shared, floating down the highway.

NOREEN MARTIN ANDOVER, OH

SET TO TAKE FLIGHT ➤

"My uncle Collins Weston is standing next to his 1954 300SL Gullwing Coupe made by Mercedes-Benz," writes Sue Weston-O'Neill of Beatrice, Nebraska. Notice the high sill below the doors that could create a challenge getting into the car. Sometime in 1957, Mercedes-Benz replaced the Gullwing with a two-seat roadster with conventional doors.

METRO MOM From Roseville, Michigan, Jean Fuller Rico writes, "I was a carhop when a girl drove up in a Nash Metropolitan. I fell in love with it!" With six children and a tight budget, a new car didn't seem possible. "By watching our money, I got my Metropolitan. All my children loved that Nash," adds Jean.

STEADY RIDE Poul Borup of Port Angeles, Washington, bought this 1959 Buick Electra in 1963 for $1,500. "It was powerful and got me through a Christmas snowstorm as I drove from Wyoming to Alberta, Canada, to visit my uncle," he says. "My uncle was surprised to see me and to see me park in a snowdrift!"

"My first bike was a 1945 Harley that had been used in World War II. Later, when I married, my husband and I bought a 1957 powder blue Harley with a sidecar as seen at right. In the photo, I'm driving a friend of mine."

LILLIAN FELDMAN LLOYD DETROIT, MI

Backtrackin'
MAKING WAY IN PLANES, TRAINS AND TROLLEYS

BY THE SEAT OF HER PANTS

Selling airplanes wasn't easy during the Great Depression, and the Taylor Aircraft Co. of Bradford, Pennsylvania, was having a difficult time staying in business. To bolster employee morale, the company offered flying lessons.

A secretary for William Piper, one of the company's investors, my mother, Mary Alice Spencer, took advantage of the offer. In December 1931, she became a licensed pilot at age 19. (That's her in the photos above with the Taylor Cub airplane.)

The flying lessons were given in the company's newly designed Taylor Cub. The lessons required far more courage than technical skill, since there was little in the way of equipment.

The airplane had no automatic pilot or radar. It even lacked a radio! There were only a few gauges and such, in addition to the stick that was used for maneuvering the airplane.

The two-seat cockpit was open, because navigation was done by sight. The main indication of losing or gaining altitude was simply the feeling in the seat of the pilot's pants!

Mom became a proficient pilot, and the attention she received wasn't lost on Mr. Piper. He recognized the advantages of having a young secretary who could fly. So it wasn't long before he had Mom ferrying parts or even airplanes to prospective buyers in nearby states.

Mom also flew to air shows to exhibit the Cub or take part in short-distance races to demonstrate the plane's abilities. At one air show, she met Amelia Earhart, who'd already become America's premier female flier.

Mr. Piper also used Mom in print advertisements in several aviation magazines. The sales pitch was simple—here was a light and affordable airplane that even a woman could fly!

Mom continued to fly and work for the company for the next six years. Then, in the spring of 1937, the plant burned down. Reopened later in Lock Haven, Pennsylvania, the company had a new owner and a new name— Piper Aircraft.

Mom made the move and worked at Piper for another year, but she never flew again. By the end of the year, a marriage license became more important to her than a pilot's license, and she started a new life as homemaker and mother.

The brief flying career of Mary Alice Spencer is part of the golden age of aviation, when life was simpler and flying was done mainly by the seat of your pants.

THOMAS SPENCER SOUTH BEND, IN

FASHIONABLE FLIGHT In 1947 folks like Jane and John Graham dressed up for a flight. Even John Jr., 2, was wearing his finest on this flight to Texas.

CLANG, CLANG, CLUNK A Sanford, Maine, trolley jumped the tracks in 1947 and nearly landed in a river. This photo means a lot to Barbara Shalhoup of Nashua, New Hampshire. She rode the trolley as a youngster, and later married the photographer!

GANDY GALS "In the summer of 1942, I tamped ties as a gandy dancer on a section crew for the Duluth, Winnipeg & Pacific Railroad," says Frances Engman Caster (left) of Culver, Minnesota. "I earned 53 cents an hour, enough money for clothes for the next school year. I also gained a good work ethic."

TURN BACK IN TIME A clear day in 1904 found a trolley full of sightseers headed to the top of Mount Lowe in California's San Gabriel Mountains for refreshments at the Alpine Tavern and a striking view from 5,650 feet. Doris Reynolds, Foxboro, Massachusetts, shares the photo from her uncle's memorabilia—he was a motorman for the Boston Elevated Railway.

Engine-nuity

These unique vehicles made lasting impressions on *Reminisce* readers. Just consider these stories and photos they share.

▲ TURN OF THE SCREW

This homemade snow machine was propelled by a screw drive, says George McCarthy of Grand Haven, Michigan. That's George behind the "wheel" with his mother beside him in this early-'20s photo. Looks as if even back then, things "augered" well for George.

▲ TAKES MOXIE TO DRIVE IT

Cars used to promote Moxie soda are still on the move. "I took this shot at a 2010 car show in Iola, Wisconsin," says Kevin Koehler of Edgar. The driver sits on the mechanical horse, and the steering wheel is in front of the saddle. "I would be terrified to drive it, since the saddle is so high," says Kevin.

➤ CATCHING A CHOPPER

"The Greyhound bus company envisioned helicopters as America's preferred method of transportation," Warren Gustafson writes from Andersonville, Tennessee. "Greyhound Skyways was established in 1946 with two four-passenger helicopters." The plan was to add landing pads to the roofs of major bus terminals. The experiment began in Detroit with the crew and helicopter shown at right. Pictured, from left, are pilots Charles Clark and Ray Browning, Sikorsky Aircraft Corp. reps Harry Nachlin and Warren, and Greyhound mechanic James Stockhecker. "Greyhound Skyways was shelved because of steep costs," Warren says.

"This unusual car was called a Stiltmobile and was built by the Eskimobile Co. During the late '20s and early '30s, when most roads were unpaved, Eskimobile made quite a few of these mud-loving machines. Some even came equipped with 'paddles' that the motorist would attach to the wheels to help pull the Stiltmobile out of sticky situations!"

DUANE MILLER ELDRIDGE, IA

▲ WAVE OF THE FUTURE?

"When my father-in-law, James Allen, was assistant cashier at the Farmers and Merchants Bank in Menomonee Falls, Wisconsin, he attended a 1961 bankers' convention in Chicago," writes Elizabeth Allen of Brooklyn Park, Minnesota. "While there, he went to the Chicago National Boat Show and saw this futuristic Evinrude Heli-Bout, a combination helicopter and outboard boat. In the photo, James is the tall young man in the dark-rimmed glasses between the 'U' and 'D' in 'Evinrude.' Although the idea is interesting, it doesn't appear that the Heli-Bout ever made it into production."

On the Road
ADVENTURESOME SPIRITS LED TO FAMILY FUN

HOT TIMES ON THE ROAD WEST

In the summer of 1959, my parents, Jim and Gerry Ringelberg, moved our family from Dalton, New York, to Arizona. There were four of us kids: Lyn, 10; me, 7; Joe, 5; and Bill, 3. My teenage cousins Phil Maker and Gary Ludwig came with us as camp hands and child wranglers, sleeping under the stars every night and taking the bus home after we reached our destination.

We traveled with two vehicles. The car was a 1955 Chevy, and the 1951 Chevy pickup had a camper in back and pulled a canvas-topped utility trailer. That's where we kids rode along with the camping gear.

We were headed for Wellton, Arizona, because Dad thought he might be able to get a farm there. Mom and Dad wanted to see the country on the way, so we were on the road for three weeks.

We saw famous sights such as Mount Rushmore, Custer's Last Stand (now known as Little Bighorn Battlefield National Monument), Yellowstone and Grand Teton parks and the Grand Canyon, and some not-so-famous ones, too. We camped in the Badlands and the Black Hills of South Dakota.

In Montana, we picked up a couple of hitchhiking cowboys. They were in the backseat of the car when a bee blew in the window and dropped between Mom's legs. She was deathly allergic and stopped the car right on the highway and leaped out until Phil got the bee out of the car.

SENTIMENTAL JOURNEY

"My aunts painted signs on both sides of our camper," Melissa Brady says. "Pictured, from left, are Dad (holding Bill's teddy bear), Lyn, Mom, Bill, me and Joe. Our cousins Phil and Gary painted over their mothers' handiwork the first night at camp."

Shortly after, a car trying to pass hit the pickup when Dad was making a left turn. No one was hurt, but there was a lot of excitement and yelling. By the time things settled down and my cousins had been sent to get an officer, we realized that our two hitchhikers had disappeared.

When we reached Arizona, our welcome to the promised land was gasoline at an outrageous 40 cents a gallon. I remember this well because of the colorful language that the price elicited from Dad.

At the Vermillion Cliffs, we closed the windows to keep out the hot wind. We thought we'd expire from the heat. We cooled right off, however, when we got to Flagstaff, where it snowed on us on July 20. Since we didn't have any warm clothes, we spent a cold, miserable night there.

We headed south, and by the time we got to Phoenix, the heat was so intense that Mom and Dad abandoned the idea of the farm at Wellton and continued to the cooler climate of Tucson, where Dad took up his old occupation of ironworking.

My parents lived in Arizona the rest of their lives, and my sister, brothers and I grew up there, but it was many years before any of us had air conditioning. I guess we were made of tougher stuff back then.

MELISSA BRADY TYRONE, NM

OH, CANADA!

I was still learning to drive in 1962 when we decided to move from Britain to Canada, adding an obstacle to my dream of acquiring a driver's license.

In anticipation of the move to North America, my husband, Jim, bought an export model Austin Cambridge for driving on the right-hand side of the road. (See photo above.) We watched the car being hoisted aboard the ship in a rope cage prior to our seven-day voyage to St. John, New Brunswick. After spending three months at a Canadian army base there, we were posted to Whitehorse in the Yukon Territory—4,000 miles to the west.

We booked ourselves onto a train from Montreal to Edmonton, Alberta. From there, we set off on the Alaska Highway, which was still a gravel road. As such, I practiced driving by maneuvering the Austin through dust clouds and over potholes.

After we arrived, I passed my driver's test in the Yukon and found there were only two seasons—winter and July. In the Yukon winter, tires freeze in the position they're left, "three-quarters round and flat to the ground," so we got used to hearing a *ker-plunk, ker-plunk* until the frozen part thawed. Gears froze, too, so we parked in reverse so we could back the car out in the morning. Despite all of this, we spent two happy years there.

Later posts included the prairies, then back east and finally Vancouver Island. The Austin lasted nearly 15 years and transported our family on lots of activities, trips and outings.

Now retired, I share a Dodge Shadow with Jim, but I often look fondly back on the miles I traveled with that Austin and a young family. That's a long time ago, because in Canada, it's all kilometers now!

ELIZABETH SYMON SHAWNIGAN LAKE, BC

SLIPPERY WHEN WET ➤

"In 1916, when I was 4 years old, my dad, Bud Schuler, and his brother Harry took a trip to Fredericksburg, Virginia, from our home in New York City," writes Frederick Schuler of St. Petersburg, Florida. "They both bought Ford Model T Roadsters and built boxes on the back for supplies. Dad even installed a spotlight at the front of his car to act as a strong headlight. In those days, rural roads had no pavement or bridges, so you drove through the streams as seen in this photo."

▲ TOP THIS

"The rig in this photograph from August 1959 belonged to my aunt and to my uncle, who is in the boat," writes John DeLaporte of Marathon, Wisconsin. "They, along with my parents, toured the U.S. in this self-contained unit. I have no idea how they loaded and unloaded the boat from the Pontiac Super Chief Custom Safari or how far they'd get down the road today before being pulled over."

▲ EARLY RV-ING

"My father and mother (far left, in 1921) often set out in their Willys-Knight touring car for an overnight camping trip with their group," writes Helen Bothwell of Sierra Vista, Arizona.

▲ ROAD READY

Virginia Grace Thurtle is standing next to her 1965 Ford Galaxie 500 with an Airstream Caravel 19-foot travel trailer attached, in 1968. "Aunt Virginia was very adventuresome," says Mary Palmer. "It was quite a club she belonged to—people who all had the same type of travel trailers."

◄ CAR COUTURE

"My great-grandmother Ethel Sexton (right) and a friend are seen in St. Louis, Missouri, between 1912 and 1918 wearing protective clothing for a car ride, which could be dusty," writes Tammie Neary of Phoenix, Arizona. "A 1915 *Ladies' Home Journal* declared that good taste, comfort and etiquette demanded correct motor togs."

Reader Favorites

MOTORISTS FACED SURPRISING SITUATIONS

HEINZ CAR GAVE LIFE VARIETY

Our two daughters were engaged in 1962, and we kept busy trying to fill their hope chests.

At the time, the H.J. Heinz Co. offered a special price on stainless steel tableware as long as you sent in a certain number of its soup labels.

My husband, John, was pastor of our Lutheran church here in Eldora. When word got around the congregation that we needed Heinz soup labels, we soon had enough to give each girl a service for eight, plus all the serving pieces!

There were a few labels left over, and I discovered an ad for a Heinz sweepstakes. All I had to do was put my name and address on the back of a soup can label and send it in. I did that with the rest of the labels.

I forgot all about it, until a private detective phoned, saying I was a potential winner. When the man arrived, he showed us his credentials and interviewed John and me. Our youngest son was absolutely thrilled to have a real detective in our very own home

On Christmas morning, I received a telegram telling me that I had won a new 1963 Ford Falcon convertible! It was one of 57 Heinz gave away, to go along with its slogan, "Makers of 57 Varieties."

With this news, we now had a dilemma. With three of five children in college, we didn't think it very good stewardship to own two cars. We talked about selling the new car, but members of our church were aghast. "Once in a lifetime you win a car and don't get to enjoy it?"

Not only were we encouraged to keep the car, but when it arrived, we were given a check to cover the taxes! The congregation had chipped in the $600.

It was a wonderful car and featured automatic transmission, a treat we'd never had. We thought it was the easiest little car to drive.

That summer, John and I celebrated our 25th anniversary, a daughter was married and another graduated from college. That was a lot of excitement for one year.

In the fall, we decided to trade in the car. It had 12,000 miles on it. With the Falcon and our other car, we got a brand-new car plus $200. It was the first time we bought a car without having to borrow money. What an incredible year 1962-'63 was!

MAE ETTA ZIMMERMANN ELDORA, IA

FAMILY CAR
The author receives the keys to her new car above. At right, daughter Ann and her husband, Dick Thompson, enjoy the convertible on a sunny day in 1963. The author's son Fred is in the back.

NOW WHERE DO I PUT THIS TICKET? "My father, Sam Pope, of the Columbus, Mississippi, police department, was issuing parking-meter citations on March 20, 1949, when he came across Fred," recalls Sam's son, Larry Pope of Fairhope, Alabama. "Fred was tied to a hitching post and it appears he was stating his position to my father. The horse apparently talked his way out of the citation but not before a reporter for *The Commercial Dispatch* newspaper happened on the scene and took the photo."

DAPPER DRESSER "My dad, Francis Bartz, always dressed sharp, as you can see in this photo taken in 1946," says Alice Buckel of Batavia, New York. "He never required a special occasion to put on his Sunday best. He also was a very devoted father who achieved his goal: To provide his children with a better life than his."

CHAPTER 9

The Way We Were

You can tell a lot about an era by its haircuts, hemlines, and icons and objects of pop culture. From bobs and beehives to mood rings and pet rocks, fads and fashions are passing fancies...but the fun they provide is everlasting.

Fashionable Flashbacks

STYLES THAT MADE US SMILE

NO SLEEP AT A SLUMBER PARTY

Much as they are today, slumber parties in the good old days were merely excuses for friends to get together. Partygoers would laugh, gossip and have their picture taken in fancy sleepwear.

This is a picture of my sister-in-law Mary Yurkzites (back row, second from right) and her friends at a slumber party near Chicago around 1924.

Back then, girls started the slumber parties when they were around 19 or 20 years old, and they continued until they started to get married.

My wife, Anne, was too young at the time to remember the names of her sister's friends. Anne does remember that Mary worked for the William Wrigley Co. in Chicago and always brought home gum to share. Anne says she turned it down because she preferred bubble gum. See? You just can't please some kids, even with free gum!

CASEY PRUNCHUNAS CHATSWORTH, CA

FIT TO BE PEGGED

Before I enlisted in the Army Air Force in World War II, I was a student at Withrow High School in Cincinnati, Ohio, class of '41.

Withrow was a large high school, and most of us dressed neatly for classes—not because we were forced to by the rules, but because we wanted to. I usually wore a shirt with French cuffs, a tie, slacks with pegged legs, saddle oxfords (dirty, of course) and my school football or track sweater.

The guys I ran around with had a favorite clothing store where you could buy dress shirts, slacks, zoot suits, ties, hats and saddle oxfords. The place was called Maxie's Pawn Shop, and although the front was a pawn shop, in back was a clothing store for men that operated by invitation only.

There were five fraternities in my high school, and during my sophomore year I became a member of Chi Omega Sigma. My school dress didn't change much, but I noticed that a lot of the other guys in fraternities wore zoot suits to the Saturday night dances. I was already an accepted customer at Maxie's, so one Saturday, a frat brother went with me to buy my first zoot suit.

The new outfit consisted of a herringbone gray coat with exaggerated shoulders. That coat almost reached my knees, and my oxford gray trousers had legs pegged so tight the tailor sewed a zipper inside each leg.

There was also a white oxford-cloth shirt with French cuffs and a button-down collar, a bright yellow knit tie, black and white saddle oxfords and a robin's egg blue hat with a 4-inch brim.

The first three days of the school week crept by because I was so eager to pick up my new outfit after school on Wednesday. I planned to wear it to our first dance on Saturday night.

When Saturday turned out to be a beautiful sunny September day, I put on my new suit and decided to walk down to Hyde Park Square so I could show it to my friend George Runte.

He owned the Frazier-Runte Hardware Store, and I considered him my first adult friend. I'd worked in his store during the summer sharpening mowers, cutting glass and waiting on customers. George had also taught me how to drive when I was 15 so I could make deliveries in his 1938 Plymouth. The customers tipped well and I saved the money, which is how I bought the zoot suit.

Walking down Erie Avenue, I stopped at a corner to wait for the traffic light to change. On the other side of the street was the Hyde Park Fire Department, and five firefighters sat out front on benches and chairs.

Then I noticed they were looking at me, nudging each other and pointing. *Guess they've never seen a zoot suit in daylight before,* I thought.

Suddenly they started laughing so hard that one of them fell out of his chair. Meanwhile, the others were dancing around and punching each other.

That's when I looked down to see a little black and white fox terrier—using my leg as a fireplug!

I'd never been so embarrassed in all my life, and the roaring laughter of the firefighters didn't help. I shook my leg and ran all the way back to my house.

It was a good thing no one was home, because this well-dressed man was close to tears. I took a shower, changed clothes and never wore that zoot suit again.

From 1942 until 1963 (from private to colonel), I wore the olive drab and the "pinks and greens" of the U.S. Army Air Force, and the blue suit of the U.S. Air Force, but I never forgot my first and only experience with a flashy zoot suit.
WILLIAM CRAMER HOPKINSVILLE, KY

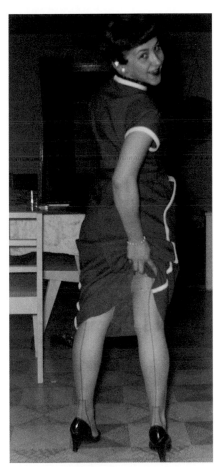

"When stockings had seams, we checked them to make sure they were straight. That's my sister-in-law Priscilla Dinehart in this 1955 photo."
GERI BITZ MULINO, OR

FOIL FINERY

Remember aluminum foil dresses? I had this one in 1968. The foil clung to my legs, so I cut the dress off at the knee.

Decked out in my foil finery, I went out for New Year's Eve with my husband, Lavon. When one of the foil ties broke, I was prepared with a roll of cellophane tape.

The dress was good for only one wearing, which was all I really wanted anyway.

BEV LEIS MILLER CITY, OH

THIS FAD WAS ALL WET

What was my friend Mary Lynn doing in the bathtub, fully clothed, when I snapped this 1962 photo?

In the late '50s and early '60s, girls on the east side of Chicago wore cutoff Levi's jeans. But the pants were available only in men's sizes at the Army store.

We'd put on the jeans, cut off the legs below the knee, then sit in a tub of hot water and wait for the jeans to shrink.

Once you emerged from the tub in your dripping jeans, you had to wear them until they dried.

MARLENE KABZA SARANAC LAKE, NY

THAT'S WHAT FRIENDS ARE FOR

I became friends with JoAnne Richards (now Davies) in seventh grade when we lived in Scranton, Pennsylvania. We're still so close that we can almost finish each other's sentences.

This photo shows me doing JoAnne's hair in 1960 after setting it on rollers. The bag on the bed held my assortment. The bangs were combed down on the forehead and held in place by special tape to make them stay in place. We also ratted or teased the hair and then sprayed it good!

JoAnne and I still get together once a year when I visit family back home, and we talk on the phone and by email. We've been friends through marriages, children, grandchildren, our parents' deaths, operations—you name it.

We are truly sisters of the heart. What a joy to know we're there for each other, and have been for more than 50 years!

SUZI ROSS BEVAN FREDERICKSBURG, VA

KEEPING IT SIMPLE

In 1945, I worked as one of the scorekeepers for North American Aviation's golf tournament, held near Inglewood, California, where the company had leased the Hollywood Park Racetrack clubhouse for the war effort.

I'm the tall woman on the far right in this photo; next to me is Imogene Booher, a close friend of mine to this day. Except for the long pants, what we wore in the picture was pretty much what we wore as workers in the purchasing department at NAA: skirts to the middle of the knee and stockings with seams down the back to keep straight.

However, nylons were next to impossible to get, so leg makeup had to suffice. Fashions were rather stark and simple during World War II, until Dior introduced the long skirt right near the end of the war, when fashions became more soft and feminine.

LORRAINE WHITTEN DARR
APPLE VALLEY, CA

BOW-TIE AFFAIR "These were the bridesmaids' dresses for the 1959 wedding of friends Nola and Ron Fox in Eldred, Pennsylvania," writes Lois Cramer of Colorado Springs, Colorado. "I'm the one at right, and Ron's sister Cherie was the maid of honor (middle). Marmie Harlan was the third bridesmaid."

STYLISH SISTERS "My sisters-in-law, Margaret (left) and Florence Rickard, are seen here as teenagers in the 1920s," says Leta Rickard of Fort Plain, New York. "Margaret became a nurse and Florence was a teacher. With their head scarves, they look like flappers."

▲ HALLWAY CHAT
"This is my mother, then Patricia Ellen Rumford, dressed in the fashion of 1959, when she was 16 years old," writes Michael DeLigio of Stateline, Nevada. "The picture was taken at her home in Neptune, New Jersey. Fifty-some years later, she still looks young after a long, happy marriage and two sons (who often tested her patience). And she still spends time chatting on the phone."

◄ FAN OF THE LONE EAGLE
"Here I am, wearing my Lucky Lindy cap in 1932 on my way home from school," says Friel Hall of Carmel, Indiana. "Charles Lindbergh was a hero to all of us American boys in those days."

➤ HIGH HEMLINES
Shorter skirts were in style at the salon where Marilyn Jacobsen (second from right) of Elmhurst, Illinois, worked as a hairdresser in the early 1960s.

▲ OVERALL, A GOOD PHOTO
"Every year, the Boss of the Road overall company gave my family new overalls in exchange for using our photo in advertising," says Charles Riise of Union City, California. "This picture was taken on our farm in Turlock, California, in 1925, when I was 5. I'm second from the right."

That's Fad-tastic

IT WAS ALL THE RAGE

PEAK PERFORMANCE

Flagpole sitting was all the rage in the late 1920s, especially in Baltimore, Maryland, and my grandfather William C. Ruppert took his turn at it.

In 1929, at the age of 14, he sat atop a flagpole for 55 days, 5 hours, 5 minutes and 5 seconds. (That's him in the photo below.)

The hero of kids in Baltimore in 1929 was Alvin "Shipwreck" Kelly, the man who originated the fad of flagpole sitting. At one time, there were about 50 kids sitting on flagpoles in the city.

My grandfather joined the fray on Aug. 1, erecting his own 20-foot pole at 627 North Point Road. "I sunk it 18 inches into our front yard," he once wrote. "At the top was a platform 18 inches wide and 56 inches long. I nailed crosspieces onto the pole for steps and went up at 2:30 one afternoon. My parents tried to get me to come down. I wouldn't."

His father eventually ran an extension cord from the house for lights and rigged up a market basket with a rope to deliver food.

"I was never lonesome," he wrote. "There was always a crowd of kids around. I read a lot of Western paperbacks. Steve Brenner came over one night, tacked up a white sheet and showed a movie for me. … I pulled up my blanket at night, tied myself to the board with a clothesline and slept well."

Older folks brought him sandwiches, pastries, candy and watermelons. A local store owner sent over a quart of ice cream every day. As a result, he gained quite a bit of weight.

In an article, my grandfather wrote, "I could have stayed a hundred days easily, but the school board had different ideas. School opened early in September, and toward the end of the month the truant officer began coming around. So on Sept. 25 at 7:30 p.m., I eased myself down a ladder, letting my arms do most of the work. My legs, so long unused, wouldn't support me. I was able to go to school in a few days, but had to walk with a cane until nearly Christmas."

During his stay aloft, my grandfather received money and gifts from supporters, along with several letters, including some from the mayor of Baltimore.

My grandfather and my grandmother Lola Ruppert lived in the Essex area of Baltimore County until his death in '68. My grandmother later moved to Bel Air, Maryland, and still lives there.

"I'm glad I did it," Grandfather wrote of his flagpole stunt. "It's a funny memory. Every man has a right to do something crazy at least once in his life."

ED KAMBERGER
ABINGDON, MD

HOPPING TO IT Fay Price (center) and her fellow carhops sported colorful outfits at Ted's Drive-In in Gary, Indiana. She can't recall the names of everyone pictured, but says the three on the left are Julie Czoka Pass, Juanita McCabe and Effie Rork. Frances Arcuri is second from right.

HARDWORKING CARHOP

Ted's Drive-In was one of the first and biggest drive-ins in Gary, Indiana. In 1951, when I was 24 with two young children, I felt fortunate to find a job there as a carhop. Ted's was easily accessible because buses ran often and on time, and I had to transfer only once.

George and Marge Pratt ran the business. They employed 15 to 20 female carhops, including my two sisters and me. The boys worked inside making sodas and handling other duties.

Marge made the striking uniforms we wore: red satin skirts and cream-colored tops. We completed the outfits with red tights, cowboy boots we bought ourselves, and majorette hats with big plumes. Everybody recognized those uniforms. The Pratts had cleaners pick up our uniforms twice a week, so we always looked great.

Ted's was known for its hot dogs, but it also served burgers, fries and the usual drive-in fare. The menu offered a nonalcoholic beverage called a Zombie, which was made with red soda pop. A sign cautioned "Limit 2," so teens sometimes thought the drinks contained alcohol and would start acting silly after drinking one. What a show!

The drive-in did a good business. Folks from Chicago would stop on their way to vacations in Michigan, so we saw a lot of people. The parking lot was huge and could hold up to five cars deep in three big parking sections.

If I walked out to a car in the back row to take an order, I would need to make at least three trips to complete the order. If the customer wanted a reorder, that was another two trips. I certainly got my exercise, and I never had to worry about my weight!

We always hoped that a reorder would mean a bigger tip. At that time, a quarter was a great tip at a drive-in. There were many nickels and dimes. If I did well, I made $7 or $8 a day. We also received a 1 percent commission on our sales. The biggest commission I ever made there was $15 for one week. Wow! That was a lot back then.

I worked there full time for two years, from 2 p.m. to midnight on weekdays and till 1 a.m. on weekends. I rarely got home before 2 a.m. That was fine when I was working just that one job. When I started working full time at Illinois Bell Telephone Co., it became rather hectic. I worked a split shift at the phone company: 7 to 10 a.m., then 4 to 8 p.m.

In between, I took a bus out to Ted's and worked five hours there. Then Marge, who was a good friend, would drive me back to the phone company. It was a good thing I was young and healthy and had a reliable baby sitter for my two young girls. But I must admit I was pretty tired all the time.

After three years of split shifts, my schedule changed at the phone company, and I had to quit working at Ted's. The drive-in went out of business shortly after. The building is gone now, and all that's left are the memories of the hard work and fun we had.

The girls who worked there have tried to stay in touch, but time and circumstances have taken their toll. There are only four I know who are still with us, including my sister Jeanne Chilelli, who lives in Phoenix. To this day, I would love to hear from any of those girls. I often think of them with a smile and wonder how they are.
FAY KEENAN PRICE
RAVENNA, OH

TWIST AGAIN ➤
"Two of our daughters' friends were playing Twister when I took this picture in our living room in 1969," says Ray Ross of Temple City, California. "We had four daughters at home in those days, and their friends were always welcome. Games like this passed the time at our house."

▲ FAMILY CIRCLES
The Burghauser children (from left), Joseph, Linda and Carol, created their own version of a three-ring circus with their toy hoops. Carol, now living in Baltimore, Maryland, shared this slide from 1958.

OUT OF CON-TROLL

When Danish woodworker Thomas Dam began crafting fuzzy-haired creatures for his daughter and her friends in 1959, he didn't realize he would spark a worldwide toy craze. But within a few years, companies copied his quirky dolls, and trollmania swept through the U.S.

Boys and girls alike went mad for these strange little beings that supposedly brought good luck to their owners. Playing off this Scandinavian tradition, one toymaker even marketed its colorful plastic trolls as Wishniks.

Kids weren't the only ones who fell under the trolls' spell: Lady Bird Johnson, who was then the nation's first lady, was among many adults who admitted to owning one of the charms.

The frenzy cooled by the '70s, but the impish dolls didn't stay down for long. In 1987, toy tycoon Russell Berrie introduced a new generation of trolls, and Hasbro toys joined the fray in the early '90s.

"My daughter, Isabelle, with a Thomas Dam troll doll that's been in my family since 1976!"

DAVID GASKELL BOLTON, UK

◄ **SERIOUS BUSINESS**
Marathon dancers like Betty and Tom Day (near left) got sponsors to pay for travel expenses to compete in marathons nationwide. "They took part in the International Championship in Philadelphia," Ted Taylor of Abington, Pennsylvania, says. At far left, a participant in another dance marathon falls asleep in her partner's arms while dancing.

THE POWER OF PRAYER

I was only 7 when the church across the street from our house started ringing its bells in the middle of a quiet afternoon.

Suddenly, the Garden Plain, Kansas, fire truck came roaring past with some of the girls from the high school hanging on, smiling ear to ear and banging on washtubs with wooden spoons.

The whole town erupted with shouting, laughter, clapping and dancing. People poured out of the stores and businesses up and down Main Street, and houses emptied in minutes. My mother stood with me on our front porch to watch the show. She noticed her cousin Lena stepping out of the front door of the church.

Lena was older than Mom. She and her husband, Fred, had five sons—four of them in the service. In those days, one son was allowed to stay home, not only to run the farm but to carry on the family name should his brothers not make it back.

Lena's farm was 7 miles out in the country, and she didn't get into town often. She, Fred and their fifth son, Francis, didn't have many comforts out there. The land was too sandy for growing anything other than watermelons.

The melons didn't help much with the income. Local boys thought it was great fun to cut the fences, stomp through her patch and take more melons than they could possibly eat.

Lena prayed for the safety of her beloved Fritz, Herman, Florian and Mike, who were fighting all over the globe during World War II. So when Lena came to town,

FOUR TIMES THE WORRY Parents Lena and Fred Linnebur were happy to have all four sons return safely from the war. Clockwise, Fritz (hatless, with an unknown serviceman), Michael, Florian and Herman became farmers.

it was not to shop but to visit the Lord and implore Him to keep her sons safe.

When Lena heard all the ruckus on that summer day in 1945, she came out of church to see what was happening. My mother ran over to hug her and say, "The war is over, Lena. The war is over."

Lena stared in disbelief. Tears clouded her eyes and she dabbed them with a handkerchief. Pulling away from Mom, she said, "Then I must go back and thank the Lord."

She disappeared back into the darkness of the church—and that touching moment remains a wonderfully poignant memory of that most momentous day.
ROBERTA LAMPE GARDEN PLAIN, KS

REMEMBERING NOV. 22, 1963

"All right, class, I want you to put away your art supplies and take out your rosaries."

Those words, uttered by my teacher Sister Eusebia, told me something was very wrong. That Friday had been an ordinary school day. I was 11 and a sixth-grader at St. Casimir School in Lansing, Michigan.

Sister Eusebia then brought out the classroom television, which was stored on a large cart. Turning the TV on but leaving the volume off, she announced that the president had been shot. We then began the 20-minute recitation of the rosary. When our prayers ended, Sister Eusebia turned up the volume, and we listened in silence.

The weekend was a blur. My parents were glued to the TV. The Saturday newspaper headlines, the nonstop news reporting about the assassination, the hunt for the killer, the capture of Lee Harvey Oswald—it was all mesmerizing.

On Sunday, to get outside for a while, my brothers and I rode our bikes to a construction site. We knew that the workers left empty pop bottles lying around. They were worth 2 cents each, so we thought we could at least make a little money that afternoon.

When we returned home, we were again stunned to hear about Jack Ruby shooting Lee Harvey Oswald and to see the replay.

There was no school on that Monday because of the president's funeral. I have vivid memories of the service, the procession with Mrs. Kennedy walking with Robert and Edward Kennedy, the riderless horse, little John Jr.'s salute to his father and the playing of taps at the grave.

Besides those terrible events of that November, I have only two recollections of John Fitzgerald Kennedy: his presidential debate with Richard Nixon and his speech about putting a man on the moon. Six years later, I saw Neil Armstrong take those first steps on the moon. And I remembered John Kennedy's words about "landing a man on the moon and returning him safely to earth."

KRISTINE KAZMIRZACK LANSING, MI

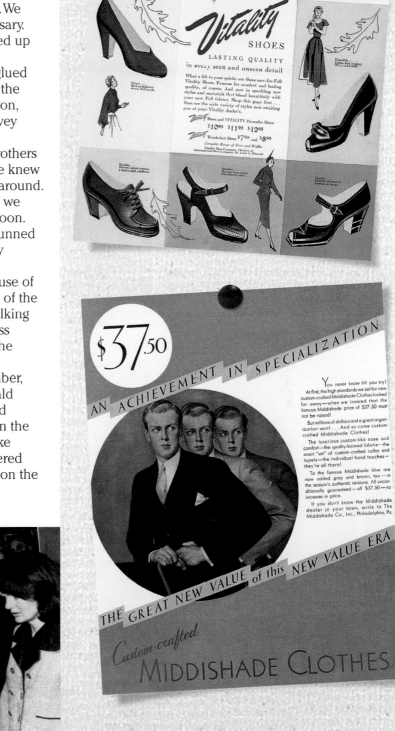

THE RIGHT STUFF

In 1961, I was serving as quartermaster aboard the aircraft carrier *USS Lake Champlain* when it recovered Cmdr. Alan Shepard and the *Freedom 7* space capsule. Launch delays had kept us waiting for several days in the recovery area, northwest of the Bahamas. (Rumor had it that Fidel Castro was jamming radio signals.) But on the morning of Friday, May 5, the 15-minute mission was a go.

The entire crew had been advised to watch the skies for the capsule as it re-entered the atmosphere, but it was the captain who first spotted its big red and white parachutes. From my station on the bridge, I had a great view of the big Sikorsky H-34 helicopters taking off, recovering the capsule and returning it to the ship.

Shepard and *Freedom 7* were flown off the ship and a dummy capsule was flown aboard and put up on the flight deck for show. Several days later, when we sailed into the naval air station at Quonset Point, Rhode Island, the crowds were there to greet us. Bands played and banners flew, and we felt as heroic as Alan Shepard himself.

PAUL PHENIX MELBOURNE, FL

CRAMPED QUARTERS Photos of the *Freedom 7* capsule—including the one above—were given to the *Lake Champlain* crew. The Mercury capsule measured 6 feet 10 inches top to bottom and 6 feet 2 inches in diameter. Each astronaut named his own capsule, adding the numeral 7 as a nod to Project Mercury's seven original astronauts.

"This shot was taken during a stop in port, probably in the Virgin Islands or Jamaica. There wasn't much for the bridge crew to do when we weren't at sea, so this was the only time we'd be allowed on deck out of uniform."

PAUL PHENIX MELBOURNE, FL

MARSHMALLOW FEAST The author (in yellow) was with brother Wayne and cousins Nancy (far left) and Eileen on the Lake Temagami island in '69.

"THE EAGLE HAS LANDED"

My summers were never boring; my father, an adventure seeker, saw to that.

In 1969, I was between high school and college. I didn't have a job, but I wasn't bored. Every year, my parents would plan trips that took my brother and me to a wide variety of destinations.

This July, we were going on a canoe trip to Lake Temagami in northeastern Ontario, Canada. The lake was in a remote, sparsely populated part of the province, about 400 miles from our home in Rochester, New York.

We packed our supplies and loaded two canoes onto the car. Along the way, my aunt, uncle and two cousins joined us.

While I don't remember most of the events of that trip, the memory of a tiny island where we camped remains. The island was really just a slab of rock with a few scraggly plants. We had chosen it as our campsite because the thick forest on the lakeshore was filled with hungry mosquitoes.

There were several things about this near-treeless island that made it a poor choice for a campsite. One was the lack of privacy. We dubbed it "No-John Island" and used a canoe to ferry over to an outhouse on shore, where there were some uninhabited cabins.

The island also was a poor place to pitch tents. The hard ground would not accept tent stakes, so we used heavy rocks to anchor the tents. Inside the tents, the slab of rock made a poor mattress, to say the least!

The most memorable event on the island happened as we huddled around my father and his small transistor radio on July 20. He was holding the radio against his ear and straining to hear the historic broadcast about Apollo 11 and the landing of the lunar module Eagle on the moon.

Radio reception was poor in our remote location, but my father could hear the dramatic details and he repeated the news to us as he heard it. The landing was not proceeding as planned, but finally the historic words were announced from the moon: "The Eagle has landed."

It was a strange experience to be camped on a remote island while we heard news from a far more remote place. We had the odd perception that we were just in our backyard, compared to the hundreds of thousands of miles that the astronauts had traveled into space.

Our island seemed more like home. We lacked comfort and privacy, but at least we had air to breathe—and gravity.

Any comparisons between our canoe trip and space exploration are presumptuous. The only thing I can say is that we were all adventure seekers who were challenged by our own adventures, and we all succeeded.

I did not accompany my family on any more trips after the summer of 1969 because I had my own adventures to experience at college and work. I'm grateful my last family adventure was a memorable one, thanks to the astronauts and a tiny island on Lake Temagami.

PATRICIA SNELL KENDALL, NY

Reader Favorites
FASHIONS AND FADS COME AND GO

THESE HATS WEREN'T FOR HOI POLLOI

My mother, Anne DeLacy, opened her millinery shop at 425 Park Ave. in New York in 1932, catering to the matrons who wore custom-designed hats. They'd bring in their mink coats, and Mother would make a mink hat to go with the coat, or a hat for any outfit.

I was so proud of her. One of her customers was Frances Perkins, secretary of labor under President Franklin Roosevelt from 1933 to 1945. Mother made tricornered hats for Madame Perkins, which were her signature hats. Mother designed them in any material to match her outfits.

She also made hats for Rosa Ponselle, a famed opera singer at that time.

The cost of Mother's hats was considerable for those days. She charged $25 to $30 for mink hats and $10 to $25 for others—when Bloomingdale's was selling hats for $4.

I remember the time a young woman returned a hat that was lime green with veiling. I told Mother I liked it, so she gave it to me to wear in the Easter parade on Fifth Avenue.

I spent quite a bit of time in the shop while I was growing up, but I wasn't very good at selling. When I was a teenager, Mom encouraged me to make a hat, but I wasn't good at that, either.

When the Park Avenue building was torn down, she moved to the first-floor level of the Hotel Barbizon for Women on Lexington Avenue. Unfortunately business declined when the bouffant hairstyle became popular and hats became passé.

ELISE BRENNEN SANTA BARBARA, CA

MILLINERY MAVEN
Anne DeLacy (above, and standing in photo with her partner, Jenny Bendheim) ran a fancy hat shop on Park Avenue in New York City.

LIFE ON CAMPUS In 1959 the students at Saint Mary's College of California set a phone booth-cramming record, a fad at the time.

MONKEYSHINES On the *Today* show set in 1953, J. Fred Muggs mugs alongside amiable host Dave Garroway.

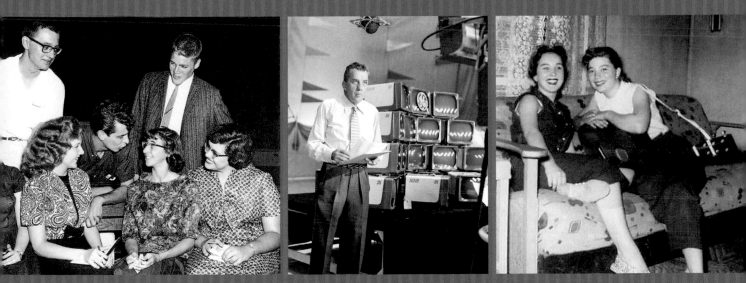

CHAPTER 10

That's **Entertainment**

❖

There's no business like show business, and that was certainly the case in the '30s through the '60s. The magic of radio and TV caught the ears, eyes and imaginations of fans across the country. Music lovers got all shook up over crooners, and a galaxy of movie stars lit up the screen. Pass the popcorn!

Stay Tuned
SAME TIME, SAME STATION

SOUNDING OFF

Huddled by the radio while growing up in Denver, Colorado, I never dreamed that one day I would enter the magical world of broadcasting myself.

That day came in the spring of 1942. I was majoring in drama at Colorado Women's College when I was hired as an actress by KLZ-CBS. I did commercials for $2 apiece and acted on a number of different radio shows. I even played opposite movie stars Victor Mature and Mark Stevens and opera singer James Melton and was directed by Bill Robson and the noted Hal Kanter.

While broadcasting, we enjoyed watching our sound effects man, Kenny Stanger, grinning as he worked. His library of recordings contained sounds like cars, birds, crickets and thunder.

Of course, things can go awry. We heard about a radio drama in which the actor shouted, "I'll shoot you!" When no gun sounded, the actor quickly said, "No, I'll stab you instead!" Then

the gunshot sounded, and he ad-libbed, "Guess I'll shoot you, too."

Noisemaking devices included coconut shells for horse hooves; a large rotating cylinder for wind; a door in a frame attached to a doorstep to mimic slamming doors and footsteps; and a sand-filled box to produce the sound of crunching snow.

For our March of Bataan show, Kenny had trouble simulating the beating of a prisoner. He finally pummeled a head of lettuce with a stick to get the desired effect.

The sound of rain was another problem. The recording we had sounded like hamburger frying. Someone said, "Fry some actual hamburger. Maybe that'll sound like rain." Kenny eventually rushed home and recorded his shower running.

We would dramatize the funnies, and when comic characters Mutt and Jeff were to be portrayed running from bees, Kenny found he had no recording of bees. We five cast members stood at the microphone and

buzzed heartily, but our lips tickled and soon someone would burst into laughter, ruining the recording. It took six takes for buzzing bees.

My variety of characters included a French freedom fighter, a Brazilian temptress, an English innkeeper, a Norwegian housewife, a Southern belle, crying and cooing babies, newsboys and even a squirrel.

One time, on *Blondie*, I played all of the women and little girls, performing eight different voices.

We once did a broadcast from the Auditorium Theatre before a live audience of 3,000 people. Kids would run up to me on the street and ask, "Aren't you Blondie?"

The voices, sounds and stories of those times still live on in my memory.

BARBARA PETERS FRENCH
ANAHEIM, CA

AIRTIME Pictured at the KLZ-CBS studios in Denver, Colorado, in all three photos is the author. Notice the soundmen in the group pictures, including Kenny Stanger (center photo, far right, with cast members).

PEDAL POWER "My grandfather Walter Mullaney was an engineer in radio and television for NBC," writes Bob Vermeulen of Glendora, New Jersey. "This 1946 picture shows him at Georgia's Augusta National Golf Club for the Masters Tournament. He had all of his equipment, including a long antenna, attached to a bicycle so he could go from hole to hole for the broadcast."

"Every Saturday morning, I would run to the mohair couch in our living room and settle down to listen to my very favorite radio program, *Let's Pretend*. I imagined what each character and scene looked like. This picture of me sitting by the Philco console with the 'green tuning eye' was taken in 1948 at our house in Elroy, Wisconsin."

MARILYN ALEXANDER ERTMAN KISSIMMEE, FL

ON TV "In 1947, my sister Ruth and I were part of the drive to send CARE packages to war-torn countries," says Marlin Toro of Campbell Hall, New York. "We were in Girl Scout Troop 236 from Brooklyn. Here, Ruth is seen with broadcaster Lowell Thomas on TV."

ED SULLIVAN: FAMILY TV

I'm sure my parents sometimes used the TV as a baby sitter, because what busy mom or dad can avoid the temptation? But it's funny: When I think back to watching TV in my 1950s childhood, I have hardly any memories of the kids shows that I'm sure I soaked up like a sponge.

What I remember is the evenings all five of us—my parents, my grandmother, my sister and I—gathered to watch shows meant for the whole family. It was always something of an event. We turned the lights down; except when a commercial came on, we would no more have held a conversation than we would have in a movie theater.

But when the show was over and we turned the lights back up, there was lots to talk about: Milton Berle's wisecracks, Dinah Shore's sunny charm, the way Sid Caesar's crazy gang chased one another over the furniture. It was entertainment that delighted three generations of us—Donna and me, with our suburban upbringing, no less than my parents, who'd grown up in East Coast cities, and my grandmother, who came from a village in Ukraine.

Best of all, though, was Ed Sullivan, ringmaster of a circus so extravagant it encompassed everything from Elvis to those famous novelty acts. To this day, whenever someone says he or she is trying to keep all the plates spinning, I picture the amazing Ed Sullivan guests who did just that—spinning multiple dinner plates, each atop its own crazily waving pole—and made it seem like magic.

In fact, before the shine wore off our first set, television itself was a little bit magical.

JOANNE WEINTRAUB MILWAUKEE, WI

MAN OF VARIETY
Ed Sullivan reviews a script on the set of his widely beloved show in 1956.

LADIES' KITCHEN BAND REALLY COOKED ON TV
Back in the '50s, a group of women from the Alum Bank area in Bedford County, Pennsylvania, used their talents in the kitchen to entertain others, have some fun and raise money for a newly formed fire department. It wasn't cooking and baking: They formed a kitchen band that featured ordinary household items used in very unordinary ways. They even rattled their pots and pans on Ted Mack's *Original Amateur Hour*.

ON-AIR EXERCISE Ethel Wall (above) hosted an exercise program in the 1950s. She also interviewed guests such as Jack Bailey, host of *Queen for a Day* (top right; Ethel is second from left), and local homemakers (right).

SHE WAS LIVE FROM OMAHA

Tap-dancing lessons from my school days in Chippewa Falls, Wisconsin, came in handy years later, in 1954, when I was the mother of four and living in Omaha, Nebraska.

I didn't want to work outside the home, so I decided to give tap-dancing lessons to the children of my friends.

I fixed up our basement by tiling the steps and a 10x11-foot area of the floor.

Shortly after I started teaching the children, their moms decided they'd like to come over at night so we could all exercise together. But it turned out the dads didn't want to baby-sit one night a week so the moms could get away, and the exercise classes ended.

A year later, while I was busy scrubbing the kitchen floor one day, a voice on our new television said, "Now, with this wonderful new medium of television, just think of all the things we can bring into the home for you!"

I thought about it for a little while. A month later, I gave an exercise program proposal to WOW-TV's station manager.

When he asked if I was going to wear revealing clothing, I said no. I designed a pair of stretch pants that tapered to just above the ankle.

The director and I spent hours selecting music for the exercises. He used records featuring Frankie Carle and his piano.

After weeks of rehearsal, I went on the air as a 15-minute summer replacement. The show was on for three months. The ladies at home liked it, and so did one of the account executives.

That led to an offer from another station, KMTV, to do a half-hour show sponsored by the Hinky-Dinky food stores. It was called *Better Living* and involved three segments: an interview, exercise, then buying groceries (from Hinky-Dinky, of course) and cooking something.

I even designed a skirt that I could wrap around my slacks and remove for the exercise segment. It was a busy schedule, but I loved it. The viewers did, too. We received thousands of letters and requests for our calorie counters.

This was great fun, but after a few years, the networks offered local stations national programming, and there was no more room for our locally produced show.

I did make one more move—to station KETV, where I hosted a show called *Charmingly Yours*. After that, I made some live commercials for weekly wrestling matches. I remember wrestler Verne Gagne often flew in from Minneapolis to appear.

All the shows I did were live. We had a big card teleprompter, but I was known for a lot of ad-libbing.

I did the programs for a total of six years and got to interview June Allyson, the McGuire Sisters and the Lennon Sisters when they were very young. I also got to meet Jack Bailey, whose *Queen for a Day* aired on KETV.

ETHEL DOUGHERTY WALL PEORIA, AZ

BIG PAYOFF IN THE BIG APPLE

Time to get up… *Clap! Clap! Clap!* By smacking his bedroom slippers together, my father followed his morning routine to wake up my mother and me.

Having spent his childhood in a rural area, my father loved big cities, so for several summers we had been spending a week in New York City. That's where we were headed in late August 1953.

We were living in Lynchburg, Virginia, where my father, Dr. H. Conrad Blackwell, was pastor of Centenary Methodist Church.

I was a senior at Greensboro College in North Carolina and had just broken up with the man who later became my husband. One of the reasons for taking me on the trip was to cheer me up.

We stayed at a hotel in Times Square and walked to Radio City Music Hall as well as radio and TV studios. We took our meals at a Childs restaurant and at a Horn & Hardart Automat to save money.

My father obtained tickets to *The Big Payoff*, a popular TV show starring Randy Merriman. Bess Myerson, Miss America of 1945, was his partner but was on vacation when we were there.

The show's format featured a male contestant who was asked four questions in his area of expertise. The correct answers won prizes for himself and a female relative, usually his wife.

My father, a shy man by nature, hesitated to fill out a contestant application, but my mother talked him into it. We were chosen to be on the show two days hence.

I don't remember what the first two questions were. The third question had to do with an obscure treaty, but my father knew the answer instantly.

The final question asked for the author of *The Power and the Glory*. My father came through again with the correct answer: Graham Greene.

We won the big payoff! The two biggest prizes were a full-length mink coat for my mother and a two-week trip to Paris for my parents. The three of us are pictured above, with the show's hosts on the right.

I fell heir to the fur coat. It has lasted until this day. Even if I no longer wear it, I will always keep it as a reminder of a happy adventure with my parents.
HARRIETT BLACKWELL HOOK
GEORGETOWN, DE

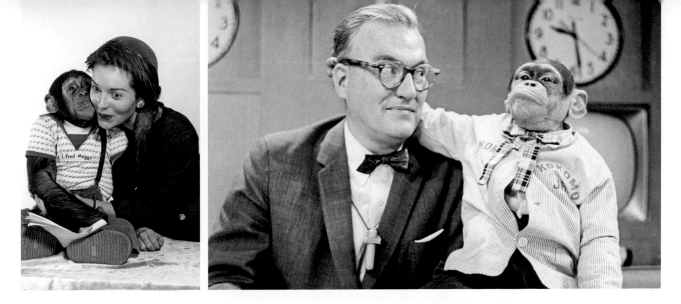

MONKEYING AROUND J. Fred Muggs goes chimp-to-cheek with a young TV reporter named Barbara Walters (above left). He was Dave Garroway's sidekick on the *Today* show (above right).

MORNING MUGGS

It is W.C. Fields who gets credit for the line "Never work with children or animals." But it might have been Dave Garroway. Sixty-some years ago, the founding host of NBC's *Today* show made the acquaintance of one J. Fred Muggs, a well-dressed 13-pound chimpanzee who was about to become his hairy little scene-stealing sidekick.

The network's morning experiment, which had debuted the previous year, was off to a slow start. The show's creator, Pat Weaver, believed he'd found an irresistible gimmick when he spotted a rascally chimpanzee on Perry Como's CBS show. Muggs made his first *Today* appearance on Jan. 28, 1953, and became a regular on Feb. 3. Weaver was right: Muggs' antics lured younger viewers to the *Today* show, and their parents followed.

The chimp served as *Today's* mascot until 1957 and became an international celebrity. Along the way, he had a "girlfriend," a more docile chimp: Phoebe B. Beebe.

When we last checked on him, the long-retired chimp was living with Phoebe in Citrus Park, Florida. Word has it he's a big fan of Matt Lauer.

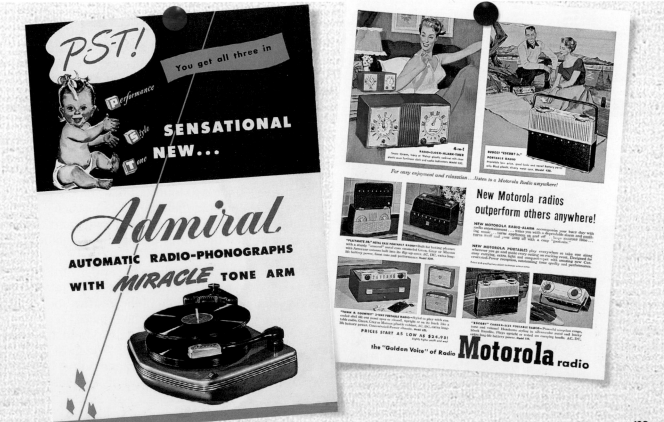

The Silver Screen
TALES FROM TINSELTOWN

JUDY GARLAND AND AUTHOR

GRETA GARBO

GENE AUTRY

SHOOTING STARS LAUNCHED HIS CAREER

Unlike many investments during the Depression, my father's paid off. He had invested in a gold mine, and with the proceeds he was able to sell our farm at Cheshire, Connecticut, in 1936 and retire to Hollywood.

It was a time of unprecedented interest in movie stars, and my younger brother and sister and I were delighted to find ourselves close neighbors to Deanna Durbin and Cecil B. DeMille! We could hardly wait to see more movie stars, so we began to camp out all day at the gates of Paramount Studios.

While most people waited with their autograph books, I held my newly acquired $1 Jiffy camera.

I still recall the first stars we saw: Gary Cooper, Mary Martin and Penny Singleton, who played Blondie. I was further delighted when they agreed to pose for this starstruck 16-year-old amateur and his little camera. What luck!

We soon found out both RKO and Columbia studios were nearby, as were the radio broadcast headquarters of NBC and CBS. Even more important, we discovered the Brown Derby restaurant, where the stars really did come out at night.

I went out nightly, too, and was rewarded with photos of Shirley Temple, Mickey Rooney and James Cagney. I was thrilled when Judy Garland posed with me for a shot!

My "night stalking" led me to buy a better camera with a flash attachment so I could shoot pictures in the dark.

Before long, I discovered I could make money selling these photos to tourists. I had wallet-size prints made and sold them for 10 cents each. I purchased a beginner's darkroom outfit and commandeered the family bathroom at night for processing and printing.

More and more stars "fell" to me and my trusty camera. I even photographed the elusive Greta Garbo, although in all three of those shots, she managed to cover all or part of her face.

My collection of star photos grew to more than 900. I sold lots of them to fan clubs. The most loyal fans were those of cowboy star Gene Autry. I had nine different poses of Gene, and his fan clubs ordered more than 500 prints!

I was so engrossed in my hobby that I neglected my schoolwork. My mother, finally giving in to the inevitable, took me out of high school and enrolled me in the prestigious Art Center School in Los Angeles so I could study photography.

The schooling paid off. After serving as a photographer in the Army Signal Corps in World War II and for a total of 10 years in the military, I became a professional photographer. For 30 years before I retired, I was the official photographer at the famous Cow Palace in San Francisco.

But through it all, I kept those fond memories of a teenage movie fan who was lucky enough to reach the stars.

HAL RANDALL MILLBRAE, CA

SHIRLEY TEMPLE

I POSED WITH THE MGM LION

I had the most wonderful experience as a teenager in 1940.

Mel Koontz, an animal trainer who specialized in movie cats, went to the editor of the *San Fernando Valley Times* in North Hollywood to suggest a publicity story.

When he asked the editor if he knew of a girl who would be willing to pose with Jackie the lion, Satan the tiger and Dynamite the panther, the editor answered: "I know just the one!" I was that girl, as he knew I loved animals. My mother was his secretary and part owner of the paper, and they later married.

I wasn't at all nervous during the photo shoot, which took about 30 minutes. I was also photographed astride an alligator, but I don't have those pictures.

The panther was the offspring of one of Frank Buck's African captives and could be recognized in movies because of one crossed eye. Jackie was in many jungle movies, including the Tarzan pictures. He was also the second and most famous of the MGM lions, roaring from within the logo for several decades.

A week after the photos were taken, my mother visited the compound at feeding time. The hungry creatures were roaring so loudly she nearly fainted dead away!

About 18 years after I posed with those beautiful cats, my husband and I took our four children to nearby Thousand Oaks to see Mel Koontz's wild animal show.

Afterward, I decided to find Mel to see if he remembered me. I spotted him alone at one of the tables, having a beer.

"Pardon me, Mel," I said to him. "I'm sure you probably don't remember me, but..."

He leaped from the chair, grabbed me and said, "Don't remember you? You were the only girl who would ever pose with my cats!"

JEANNE LITTLE SALEEN SAN CLEMENTE, CA

◄ IT'S SHOWTIME, FOLKS!

Lewis Corson was wearing a different sort of uniform when he got out of the service after World War II. "When I returned, I was hired as a doorman by the Paramount Theatre in Lynn, Massachusetts," Lewis says. "I had worked there as an usher in high school. This photo was taken in 1946, as I recall. On the bill at the time was a movie starring Alan Ladd and Veronica Lake. A ticket was 25 cents. The reason for the photo was a promotion, some kind of giveaway the theater was having that day. Notice all the ladies in fur coats, and most of them are wearing hats." Lewis ended up not making a career out of the theater. He was recalled into the Army for the Korean War. After that, he made the Army a career and retired with 33 years of service.

SPELLING IT OUT ►

"My first job, in 1947, was as a 16-year-old usherette at the RKO Uptown Theatre in Highland Park, Michigan," says Barbara Sharpe of Mountain View, California. "It was a 20-minute bus ride from Hazel Park, where I lived. This picture shows us in our usherette uniforms, advertising the movie *Gilda*; I'm carrying the G. The police even stopped traffic as we marched down the middle of the street a few blocks. All of that attention must have worked, because we were really busy at the premiere of that movie!"

Our Music

STARRY-EYED Author Jane McCarthy could only smile as singer Freddy "Boom Boom" Cannon gazed into her eyes at the 1959 Michigan State Fair. She and the other teens were honored guests.

'59 STATE FAIR WAS TEEN'S DREAM COME TRUE

Throughout the 1950s, the end of summer meant the beginning of the Michigan State Fair. Attending the fair was a cherished ritual, and I *never* missed one.

I'd always enjoyed the animal barns, the butter sculptures and the merry-go-round, but as I got older, my expectations for the fair changed a bit.

In 1959, the attraction I most wanted to see was the rock 'n' roll show hosted by Dick Clark. I was about to enter high school in Dearborn, a Detroit suburb, and rock 'n' roll ruled my life.

Then I heard about a contest sponsored by *The Detroit Times* in which teenage readers submitted essays about the lineup of stars. The winners would be honored guests on opening day of the fair, and they would actually get to meet all the stars.

There would be six winners, and I was determined to be one of them. Pen in hand, I assembled my thoughts and added some creative illustrations.

My efforts paid off. I was among the victorious—and the payoff was unreal!

On opening day, the six of us rode in Corvette convertibles in a parade down Detroit's main thoroughfare. But the best part was getting to meet the stars.

We had photo sessions with Frankie Avalon, Bobby Rydell, Jan and Dean, Santo & Johnny, Freddy Cannon and Dick Clark. We met and got autographs from the Coasters, LaVern Baker, Duane Eddy, Jack Scott, Anita Bryant, Skip & Flip, Dick Caruso and Rusty York. All of these performers were teen idols. I had their 45-rpm hit records at home, stacked right next to my hi-fi.

During the show, the winners were seated in a special area and received souvenir programs. I must have looked like the cat that swallowed the canary. What would all those screaming girls think if they knew that only two hours earlier, I'd been standing on the steps of Frankie Avalon's trailer and that I was now holding the exact same pen with which he'd signed my autograph book? Was I cool or what?

The butter sculptures and merry-go-round charmed me for years. But in the waning days of summer, when it's time for the state fair, those aren't the things I remember most.

It's a group of six giddy teenagers, mesmerized by the once-in-a-lifetime event we shared in the summer of 1959. For me, it was a perfect ending to a remarkable decade.

JANE WHITE MCCARTHY LIVONIA, MI

I RODE GENE AUTRY'S HORSE

My mother, Dorothy Provenza, managed the music/record department at McCrory's department store in Shreveport, Louisiana, for most of the 1940s.

While the department was owned by a New York company that leased the space from McCrory's, it was commonly referred to as Dottie's Music Department.

Shreveport was a very nice, clean city of around 100,000 people, and I was pretty free to roam through most of it at will while my mother was at work.

Any time I got bored or had a reason to go downtown, I would just board a trolley and hang out at McCrory's.

Mother always had one or two storefront windows decorated with the theme of a current hit song or a performer who was scheduled to be in Shreveport. She called musical artists and movie stars who were coming to town and asked them to stop by her store to sign sheet music, photos or album covers.

Her store became quite popular and everyone knew that if a star was coming to town, he or she would probably come to the store. Consequently, they watched the local newspaper for details.

In 1948, when I was 11 years old, my hero was Gene Autry. When Mother found out he was coming to perform at our local auditorium, she called him at home at his Melody Ranch in California's San Fernando Valley and asked if he would consider visiting her store.

He was very nice and said that since she had gone to the trouble of calling him long-distance, all the way from Shreveport, he would certainly be there.

McCrory's storefront was on Texas Street, the city's big, wide main street. Directly across Texas Street was the courthouse,

COWBOY STAR Gene Autry (in white hat) and songwriter Johnny Bond (gray hat) visited with author (plaid shirt) and mom Dottie (black dress).

which took up a full city block. A popular entertainment then was parking your car on Texas Street and watching the people go by, getting out occasionally to window-shop.

When the big day arrived, most everyone assumed that Gene would park in front and come in one of the two front doors. The manager, Mr. Bolen, who was a really nice man, offered to let me cover the rear door in case he came in from the alley.

Shortly, to my surprise, a big Cadillac came down the alley and stopped, and Gene Autry and singer/songwriter Johnny Bond got out.

Since I was the only one at the door, they asked if this was the place they were seeking.

I could hardly talk, but said "Yessir" and led them into the store and to Mother's area.

There was a large crowd in the

store by then, with most of the managers still at the front doors. I guess I felt pretty important leading Gene and Johnny through that crowd.

Gene and Johnny were both very nice and must have stayed for about an hour, signing autographs, pictures and sheet music and talking with the crowd.

The next day, when Mother and I went to the auditorium, a horse trailer was parked in front and a man was leading Gene's horse, Champion, from the trailer onto the sidewalk.

When I ran over to get closer, the man asked if I would like to ride Champion up the steps to the front door. What a thrill!

The show was great, and I guess you can tell by the photo of us inside the music department (above) that it was a while before reality set in for me.

EDMOND SMITH LITTLE ROCK, AR

LADY DJS WERE A BIG HIT

The seventh floor of the Bank of America building in San Diego housed a large collection of records and several young "merry maids of music" to play them back in the '40s and '50s.

The operation was called "Choice By Voice." Restaurants, nightclubs, USOs and YMCAs had jukeboxes that had a girl's voice asking for the record request when a coin was dropped in. The requests then came to us through a switchboard. We'd find the records and then put them on a turntable.

We had a huge inventory of records (that's me posing with some below), and as many as 16 or 17 turntables going at once. It took months to learn the inventory, where records were filed by number. It was like trying to learn the telephone book!

It was fun, though, and we liked it when songs from the show *Your Hit Parade* were played over and over. That way we learned the lyrics and could sing along.

There are four of us still around who worked there, and we still get together for lunch and reminisce about our days as "disc jockeys."

JUNE MITCHELL SAN DIEGO, CA

SHE TURNED DOWN ELVIS!

In the mid-1950s, my best friend and I performed on *The Louisiana Hayride*, which started as a radio show on KWKH in my hometown of Shreveport. Carolyn Bradshaw (above left) and I (right) were 17.

I had been touring with Paul Howard and His Arkansas Cotton Pickers, from the Grand Ole Opry, and Johnny Horton.

One day I called Carolyn, and she said excitedly, "You'll never guess who I'm dating! Elvis!"

Never having heard of Elvis, I asked, "Who?"

"Don't tell me you haven't heard of Elvis Presley?" she said.

"I'm afraid not, but the name is enough to choke a horse," I said.

"He's a cat!" Carolyn replied, meaning he was a cool cat—he played the kind of music that wasn't the three-chord Hank Williams songs we played, and he moved around onstage.

One day Carolyn and I were in the basement office of Pappy Covington, the booking agent for *The Louisiana Hayride*. Stars and musicians gathered in Pappy's office at all hours of the day.

This time Elvis was there. He kept trying to discreetly put his arm around my chair, then my shoulders. I gently moved his arm, and a couple of the guys giggled.

After this happened a few times, I threw his arm from around me and told him, "Listen, Elvis. You keep your hands to yourself."

That brought guffaws from the musicians, because girls just did not refuse Elvis' advances!

I didn't like him at the time because of his language and cockiness—and in my mind he'd just murdered "Blue Moon of Kentucky." After Col. Tom Parker started managing Elvis and taught him how to behave, he was a perfect gentleman when we played our package shows. We performed together all over the country.

I loved knowing him and performing in shows with him.

I suppose I may be the only girl to turn down Elvis.

NITA LYNN-ZAHN SHREVEPORT, LA

LUNCHTIME WITH THE FAB FOUR

Although I have lived in the States for 38 years, I was lucky enough to see the Fab Four perform in Liverpool before they became famous.

In 1962, the Cavern Club held lunchtime sessions. And because it was our school holiday, my best friend suggested we go. I was 13 at the time and had a strict father, so it was impossible for me to go to any club at night. But my pal, two grades ahead and running with a racier crowd, was always up for anything. So I just tagged along in her wake.

Three of us met in the ladies room at the Lime Street train station, a fabulous setting for getting dolled up since it had a whole wall of gigantic Victorian mirrors. Armed with ice-pink lipstick and gooey foundation, we put ourselves together using eye shadow, liner and that awful block mascara you used to have to spit in before brushing it on.

Satisfied, we headed off arm in arm, with our back-combed classic beehives held with hair spray so strong it would have kept a head of dandelion tufts intact in a hurricane. As we joined the line outside the entrance, my friend warned me not to open my mouth to the doorman in case he guessed my age. (You were supposed to be 18.) I nodded, smiled and handed him the entrance fee, quaking in my stiletto shoes.

Tickets in hand (they were less than 50 cents), we trooped down the steps, emerging into a dank, brick-lined cellar divided into three low tunnels with spotlights illuminating a central stage. Rows of seats were arranged in the main area, but we chose to sit at one of the tables along the left aisle so we could dance.

The place had a dim, seedy feel to it, and I quickly realized I had to be the youngest kid there.

Lighting up a cigarette, I crossed my legs and tried to look cool sipping a Coke, even though it was packed and hot, the walls now running with condensation. I was dying for a boy to ask me to dance before my beehive drooped from the humidity.

Then the announcer took the mic, welcoming the Beatles and informing the restless customers that Ringo Starr from Rory Storm and the Hurricanes would be sitting in for this performance; drummer Pete Best had called in sick.

Starting off with an up-tempo version of "Red Sails in the Sunset," the gig was soon rocking. Although we had never heard of the Beatles, they were an instant hit with the crowd that day, the four lads exuding a wonderful charisma and confidence.

The side aisles were filled with patrons dancing to their addictive, driving rhythms. My two companions thought Paul looked cute. I was attracted to bad boys and found myself irresistibly drawn to John's intensity.

George, a much quieter, gawky kid with thicker hair, also fascinated me.

Ringo, the skinny stand-in drummer, sported a homely grin as he kept the beat to the Little Richard numbers.

Everyone was mesmerized. During that session they did not play any of their own material, just covers.

I arrived home bubbling with excitement after hearing my first live rock 'n' roll performance, hoping John would fill my dreams that night and never once thinking that these four young musicians would become so celebrated.

HILARY E. BARTLETT
BOOTHBAY HARBOR, ME

FAN GIRL Hilary Bartlett (right) and her friend show off a Beatles haircut and a beehive 'do in the summer of 1962.

We Knew Them When

OUR BRUSHES WITH FAME

SIGN OF GREATNESS

When I was a kid, summertime meant Little League baseball, day camp, the Philadelphia Phillies and occasional family trips to the New Jersey shore.

One day, my father said we were taking a trip to New England to visit an artist. I was aghast.

But my dad, who was a family physician with a longtime interest in art, was writing a book about this gentleman and had set up an appointment to interview him.

On the five-hour drive, I grumbled as I flipped through my baseball cards. I wondered how the players would feel on this trip.

We finally arrived at a little town nestled in the Berkshire Mountains of far western Massachusetts. After lunch, we went to the artist's studio.

A tall, lanky, elderly gentleman cheerfully greeted my mom and dad. He asked who I was, and my father said, "This is our son Brad, who wanted to meet you." I thought, *Wanted to meet you?*

We were ushered into the studio, and I looked around, admiring the sunlit room with a big easel in the middle. All around were tubes of paint, empty juice cans full of brushes, interesting props hanging from the rafters and the walls, and several sketches lying on his desk. I quickly noticed that the man was a good artist.

Following the interview, the artist turned to me and asked, "Who's your favorite baseball player, Brad?"

"Well," I replied, "for the Phillies, Mike Schmidt or Pete Rose. Otherwise, I guess Hank Aaron or Brooks Robinson."

"Brooks Robinson," he said. "I painted his picture signing a baseball for a little boy."

I nearly jumped out of my chair.

"As a matter of fact," he continued, "I have a print of it."

He walked over to a large cabinet and pulled out a poster-size print. "Would you like it?"

"Wow! Sure!" I exclaimed. "Thank you!" And he signed it.

Soon after, we said goodbye. I almost didn't want to leave.

Later, my father said, "Brad, you just met an American legend, and now I'll show you why."

We walked to a big white house. Inside was a museum. Large oil paintings were on every wall, each more beautiful than the one before. This wasn't boring art.

There were magazine covers, story illustrations, advertisements, portraits of famous people and pen-and-ink sketches.

Many years later, I met Brooks Robinson. He too signed my picture—next to the signature of my pal Norman Rockwell.

BRAD STOLTZ PHILADELPHIA, PA

WINNING CONNECTION
The author and parents Don and Phyllis Stoltz visited the office of the famed artist, who signed the print above, as did Brooks Robinson.

CHILDHOOD DREAMS Shy Marguerite, on Shirley's left, was mesmerized in the star's presence. Shirley's mother set 56 pin curls every night to achieve those iconic, perfect ringlets.

MEETING SHIRLEY TEMPLE

Shirley Temple was my childhood idol. Her bouncy ringlets and cheerful smile made even the darkest days of the Depression seem a little brighter. When she passed away, in February 2014, the sad news brought back a flood of memories—especially of one unforgettable event.

Growing up in the Los Angeles area, my sisters and I were huge Shirley fans. We saw many of her films at Grauman's Chinese Theatre in Hollywood and played with paper dolls made in her likeness. I even had my own Shirley Temple doll.

Early one December morning in 1937, when I was 10, our grandmother woke us up and said we'd be taking a streetcar to Hollywood. She did not, however, tell us why.

Our parents belonged to a local group for people of Swiss heritage, and because *Heidi* had recently opened, a lucky group of kids of club members received invitations to meet the child star.

Our mother was in the hospital, having just given birth to our sister Catherine, so our grandmother dressed Dorothy, Pauline and me in our Sunday best and herded us out the door.

We learned the reason for all the secrecy only once we arrived at the gates of the 20th Century Fox studios. To our astonishment, our grandmother told us we were going to meet Shirley Temple!

The actress, then just 8 years old, had a private bungalow on the studio lot where she and her mother lived when she was making a film. All the furniture was sized to fit her, including a desk, a white phone and a very small grand piano.

As we stepped across the threshold, Shirley greeted our group and showed us around.

I was so mesmerized I couldn't let her out of my sight.

Later, we went outside and stood in line to play on Shirley's wooden swing. We were supposed to have lunch with her, too, but the studio hadn't counted on such a large group, so instead we were served cake and ice cream.

We did, however, get to take a group snapshot together—and I stood right next to my idol! I don't remember saying anything in particular to the star that day, though. I was much too shy.

Shirley lifted our nation's spirits during a most difficult time, and Americans continued to embrace her long after the end of her Hollywood career. I'm proud I got to meet her.

MARGUERITE BRISBIN TORRANCE, CA

HITCHED "On Dec. 31, 1947, Roy Rogers and Dale Evans appeared at the Sulphur County Courthouse in Oklahoma for a marriage license," says Ruby Plumlee. "Mabel Fulton (second from left) was county clerk then; she lived across the street from my parents, J.C. and Emma Chandler."

DUBBED In 1957, Robert Mitchum flawlessly read his lines for the radio show *Across the Blue Pacific*. But John King (right) of Wauwatosa, Wisconsin, who also acted in the show, recalls, "I was so nervous, I had to return later and dub my lines in a calmer voice."

ONE LUCKY GUY "I was working as a lifeguard at The Breakers in Palm Beach, Florida, on Jan. 13, 1927, when I had to rescue a man I'd warned not to swim in the rough waters," says Austin Wetherell of Leesburg, Florida (center). "The man, Mont Tennes of Chicago, was so grateful he gave me $1,000, a 1928 Pontiac and $100 a month so I could return to school. I was training for the Olympic swimming team at the time, but I quit that and my job as a lifeguard and went back to school. I kept swimming, though. I even taught Fred Rogers of *Mister Rogers' Neighborhood* fame to swim. We stayed in touch for years." That's young Mr. Rogers to the left of Austin.

A MEMORABLE DAY AT RKO

My father was a claims adjuster who handled a good many claims for RKO Radio Pictures. As a courtesy, he received permission for us to attend a filming at the RKO set in April 1946.

We watched the scene from *Sinbad the Sailor* in which Douglas Fairbanks Jr., as Sinbad, entertains Anthony Quinn and the beautiful Maureen O'Hara with his magic tricks. The scene was shot many times because the blue smoke covering the magic act befuddled Mr. Fairbanks so much that he kept forgetting his lines.

Finally, when the take was over, Miss O'Hara came over and joined us for this photo. Pictured from left are my father, W.H. (Bill) Freeman; my mother, Genevieve (Gene); Miss O'Hara; Pasadena's 1946 rose queen, Mary Rutte; and me, then a 16-year-old high school senior.

Miss O'Hara was so very gracious, visiting and laughing with us for some time while a new scene was set up. I'll never forget admiring her costume. She told me that with all the jewels and underskirts, the dress weighed 40 pounds!

JACQUE SUTPHIN VANCOUVER, WA

SIX GALS AND A GOV

When I was a youngster, we lived in the small town of Eureka, Illinois. One Saturday afternoon in September 1941, actor Ronald Reagan paid a surprise visit to his alma mater there, Eureka College.

Though unprepared for his arrival, the college wanted to take advantage of a photo opportunity with its Hollywood-star alumnus (and future California governor and U.S. president) and rounded up some coeds for this picture. As you can see, they were already preparing for their Saturday night dates.

A friend of my dad's took this picture, possibly as a freelance job for the college.

RUTH FARISS HARTFORD, WI

Reader Favorites
GOLDEN MEMORIES

WATER NYMPH

There it was, the most beautiful sight I'd ever seen in my young life: a green island afloat on the bluest water as our chartered plane headed in to land at the José Martí International Airport in Havana, Cuba.

As I drifted off to sleep later that night, after having taken part in a festive carnival parade through the streets, I reflected on how I came to be a part of the S.S. Water Follies, a first-class water ballet and stage show.

In 1949 I was a 21-year-old from a small town in Iowa, but in the few years before that I had lived in Chicago, New York and Boston. This time, adventure came to me while I was working as a cocktail waitress at Boston's Hotel Touraine.

Sam Snyder, producer of the S.S. Water Follies show, was seated at one of my tables. After noticing my athletic shoulders, he said, "My show needs more swimmers. How would you like to go to Havana?"

Would I ever! Hollywood glamorized Latin American countries in the 1940s, so I was definitely interested. I passed a requisite swimming test and the very next day took a train to New York, where rehearsals were already in progress.

Seventeen other girls and more than a dozen other people were involved in the show. I was probably one of the few girls hired for her actual swimming ability, but I was clueless onstage.

The show's director was an impatient man, and after I turned the wrong way four times in one rehearsal number, he fired me.

Fortunately, Mr. Snyder was in the room, and I was soon back in the chorus line. But from that point on, I was in the back row.

After our week in New York, then a stop in Miami for dress rehearsals, we arrived in Havana. The show had brand-new costumes and a live orchestra performing in an old bullfighting ring.

We danced onstage and at a certain point peeled off our plumed headdresses and sequined costumes to reveal golden yellow swimsuits and rubber swim caps. Floating on my back in starburst formation with the other girls was one of the best parts, especially when we all slowly sank to the bottom of the pool with legs held high, toes pointed to the Caribbean sky. I don't recall seeing an empty stadium seat once in our six-week run.

On my first day in Havana, I met a tall Cuban man named Willie (pictured with me) who spoke English

and looked a lot like American actor Dana Andrews. Willie had been hired as the water show's master of ceremonies, and he immediately asked me out on a date.

He was a brilliant dancer who loved taking me to Havana's nightclubs. We often lunched at the Havana Yacht Club, and I swam in the pool at the Hotel Nacional. At that age, I had no problem doing one or two shows a day, then dancing into the night.

After several months in Havana, the producers announced that they had a contract for us to perform in Caracas. I reluctantly said goodbye to Willie. After Venezuela I left the show and went to Chicago, where I met my future husband.

In 1959, I sadly watched Castro's takeover of Cuba in the news. A year later, I received a phone call from Willie: He was married with two daughters, and had managed to escape from Cuba.

There was a time when I wanted to return to Cuba, but that time has passed. Still, when I hear a tune from *South Pacific*, the show's music, I dream of the aquacade backstroke under the Cuban moon.

PAULA HASSLER TEMPE, AZ

TRUE DEVOTION Screaming fans mob an Elvis Presley concert in Florida in 1956 while police officers attempt to keep them under control. The frenzy Elvis inspired when he revolutionized the music scene will forever make him rock 'n' roll's first true star.

25 Favorite Covers
REMINISCING THROUGH THE YEARS

HATTIE'S HATPIN IS ON PAGE 167, ON THE FAR LEFT BETWEEN THE WHITE BUILDINGS.